PUMPKIN PAINTING

PUMPKIN PAINTING

Jordan
McKinney

Sterling Publishing Co., Inc.   New York
A Sterling/Chapelle Book

FOR CHAPELLE:
Jo Packham, Owner
Cathy Sexton, Editor
Staff: Malissa Boatwright,
    Rebecca Christensen,
    Amber Hansen, Holly
    Hollingsworth, Susan
    Jorgensen, Susan Laws,
    Amanda McPeck, Barbara
    Milburn, Pat Pearson,
    Leslie Ridenour, Cindy
    Rooks, Cindy Stoeckl,
    Nancy Whitley
Designers: Renee Coles, Kathy
    Frongner, Holly Fuller,
    Sharon Ganske, Tammy
    Johnson, Jamie Pierce,
    Phillip Romero, Alison
    Timothy, Amy Williams
Kevin Dilley, Photographer
Hazen Photography

If you have any questions or
comments or would like
information on specialty
products featured in this book,
please contact Chapelle, Ltd.,
Inc., P.O. Box 9252, Ogden, UT
84409 • (801) 621-2777 •
(801) 621-2788 Fax

10 9 8 7 6 5 4 3 2 1

Paperpack edition published 2001 by
Sterling Publishing Company, Inc.
387 Park Avenue South, New York, NY 10016
© 1996 by Chapelle Ltd.
Distributed in Canada by Sterling Publishing
c/o Canadian Manda Group, One Atlantic Avenue, Suite 105
Toronto, Ontario, Canada M6K 3E7
Distributed in Great Britain and Europe by Chris Lloyd at Orca Book
Services, Stanley House, Fleets Lane, Poole BH15 3AJ, England.
Distributed in Australia by Capricorn Link (Australia) Pty. Ltd.
P.O. Box 704, Windsor, NSW 2756 Australia

Printed in Hong Kong
All Rights Reserved

Sterling ISBN 0-8069-5871-5

TABLE OF CONTENTS

THE BASICS
BEFORE BEGINNING

This book was created for the painting enthusiast to take the art of painting to a new dimension. The young and the old can enjoy transforming ordinary gourds into incredible works of art!

THE GOURD FAMILY

Pumpkins are part of the gourd family, as are melons and squash. Pumpkins and melons, however, are considered to be fruit, and all varieties of squash are considered vegetables.

All gourds have a thick, tough skin. Painting, carving, and embellishing can be done in the same manner on any variety.

Gourds are grown in several colors, including various shades of orange, yellow, green, brown, and white. Try picking a gourd in a color that will eventually be the background color for the chosen artwork. This will eliminate a base coat.

Because of the unusual shapes in which many gourds can be found, creativity is unlimited. Refer to photos on pages 15 and 37. Try turning a pumpkin on its side and use the stem as part of the design. Refer to photos on pages 19 and 20.

Because of the varying sizes of gourds (especially pumpkins!), the patterns provided can easily be adapted to fit any size. Once a determination has been made regarding the general size of the gourd to be used, a photo copy can be made of the pattern in either an enlarged or a reduced state.

CHOOSING THE PERFECT PUMPKIN

When using a fresh pumpkin for painting, choosing one that will suit the chosen pattern is very important. When choosing one for carving, it is important that the complexity of the design be taken into consideration. Match more difficult designs to large, smooth, and/or flat pumpkins.

Always use fresh pumpkins that are free from bruises and never purchase a pumpkin that does not have a stem. Once a stem has been broken off, the pumpkin will not last long. If a pumpkin can be chosen and picked from the vine, try to leave two to three inches of vine on the stem. This will allow the pumpkin to stay fresh longer.

Remember that once a pumpkin has been carved, its life expectancy is only two to five days.

EXTENDING THE LIFE OF THE PUMPKIN

Pumpkins are considered seasonal fruit and, therefore, fresh ones cannot be found year around. Fresh pumpkins can be stored for several months under controlled conditions. They must always be kept dry and cool, and must not be allowed to freeze. When storing pumpkins, keep space around each pumpkin so that air can circulate. Never stack them — if one should get a rotten spot, it could infect the entire pile!

In case fresh pumpkins cannot be found, the general instructions provided include tips for painting on plastic pumpkins, compressed styrofoam pumpkins, papier-mâché pumpkins, and pumpkins made from wood, as well as for painting on fresh pumpkins.

GENERAL INSTRUCTIONS FOR PUMPKIN PAINTING

The idea of painting on pumpkins is a relatively new one, and it has allowed pumpkins to be used in a new art form. Pumpkin painting should be kept simple, yet complex enough to keep imaginations busy!

PREPARING PUMPKINS FOR PAINTING

Because of the nature in which pumpkins are generally purchased, fresh pumpkins should be thoroughly washed and dried before patterns are transferred onto them.

BASE-COATING PUMPKINS

Sometimes a pumpkin will be painted with a design and the background will be left as the unpainted surface of the pumpkin. In some cases however, the pattern requires that the entire pumpkin surface be painted. Acrylic paints have been used on the projects in this book and the number of coats necessary will be determined primarily on the base-coat color being used. If available, spray paint can also be used to base-coat pumpkins.

When fresh pumpkins are being used, a paint sealer should be used on the entire pumpkin surface before acrylic paint is applied. This will help adhere the paint to the surface. If a paint sealer is not used, paint can easily chip off. Because the surfaces of plastic, compressed styrofoam, papier-mâché, and wooden pumpkins are rough and porous, a layer of paint sealer is not usually necessary.

TRANSFERRING PATTERNS ONTO PUMPKINS

The pattern must first be adapted to a size that will work with the size of pumpkin being used. A photo copy, enlarged or reduced appropriately, is the easiest way to assure the design will be in proportion to the size of the chosen pumpkin. If all the colors in the pattern are dark, a color copy may be necessary to get the line definition needed for pattern transferring.

• METHOD ONE

The pattern can be traced onto tracing paper and then transferred onto the pumpkin using graphite paper. Place the graphite paper between the pattern and the pumpkin with the graphite side facing the pumpkin. Tape the graphite paper and the pattern into position. Carefully, but firmly, trace the pattern using a pencil. Lift the corner slightly to make sure the pattern is transferring nicely. Once the design has been transferred, remove the pattern and the graphite paper.

• METHOD TWO

Make a photo copy of the pattern and cut it out. Place it on the pumpkin and tape it into position. Carefully trace around the pattern. When using a fresh pumpkin, use a dull pencil or a blunt object and press hard enough to make a slight indentation on the pumpkin's surface, but be very careful to not puncture it. Once the design has been transferred, remove the pattern.

PAINTBRUSHES & SPONGES

Paintbrushes are the most common tools used for painting pumpkins and good quality synthetic brushes work best when using acrylic paints. Sponges should be used when sponge painting and can be found in many different sizes and textures.

A variety of different sized paintbrushes are recommended — the size of the brush will depend upon the size of the pattern you are painting. Small, liner brushes are used for detailing and large, flat brushes are used for painting larger areas, such as base-coating. Flat chisel blenders, scrollers, and shaders might also come in handy, but are not mandatory.

BASIC PAINTING TECHNIQUES

Solid base-coating is done by applying two to three coats of acrylic paint. This will give the best coverage and an even look to the paint.

When base-coating with a "wash," add water to the acrylic paint to achieve a sheer color. The amount of water used will determine the intensity of the color. When applying a wash, work as quickly as possible, using long, even strokes, but do not overlap.

Sponge painting is done by loading the top of a sponge with paint. Blot the sponge on a paper towel until most of the paint has been removed. Apply the paint to the pumpkin by lightly "blotting" the sponge up and down. Work in a circular motion starting at the center of the pumpkin.

Highlighting and shading is done by dipping a flat brush in water and then removing the excess water from the brush by blotting it on a paper towel. Apply acrylic paint to the side of the flat brush and blend, staying in one track, until the paint fades evenly across the brush. The paint will fade from dark to light.

Dry brushing is done with a flat brush dipped in a small amount of acrylic paint. Remove the excess paint from the brush by working in a criss-cross motion on a paper towel. Using the same motion, lightly apply the paint to the pumpkin.

Always allow acrylic paints to dry thoroughly before applying additional coats or colors. When a quicker drying time is necessary, a blow dryer can be used to aid in drying the paint.

If mixing colors is necessary to get a perfect shade, mix a sufficient amount to complete the project. Excess paint can be stored in airtight containers.

DETAIL PAINTING & OUTLINING

The experience of the painter usually determines how the pumpkin will be detailed and outlined. Painter's with a great deal of detail painting experience most generally opt to detail paint using a liner brush. Painter's with little or no experience will want to use a fine- or medium-point permanent marker.

When using a liner brush, load in paint thinned with water. Pull the brush through the paint, turning as you go to get a fine point. Hold the brush perpendicular to the work and line the desired areas. The thickness of the line will be determined by the amount of pressure applied to the brush.

SEALING THE ARTWORK

After the artwork is complete and the paint is completely dry, it is recommended that an acrylic spray sealer be used to set the paint and protect the artwork. Either matte sealer or gloss sealer can be used depending on the look that is desired.

GENERAL INSTRUCTIONS FOR PUMPKIN CARVING

Pumpkin carving has been enjoyed for many, many years and, therefore, is briefly included in this book. Keep in mind that a painted pumpkin can also be accented with carved sections and some of the patterns provided can be used as patterns for simple carvings!

PREPARING PUMPKINS FOR CARVING

An opening in the pumpkin needs to be cut. Using a large, sharp knife, cut out the top for a lid or cut out the bottom of the pumpkin. Cut the lid out at an angle. This provides a ledge for the lid to rest on. For easy alignment, cut a "key" in the lid so that replacing the lid is simpler.

"Key" cut in lid of pumpkin

It is recommended that the lids on smaller pumpkins (less than 10" diameter) measure approximately 4" in diameter and the lids on larger pumpkins (more than 10" diameter) measure approximately 6" to 8" in diameter.

Once an opening has been cut, the seeds and the inside membrane need to be cleaned out. Scrape out the inside lining of the pumpkin until the walls are approximately 1" thick.

TOOLS NEEDED FOR PUMPKIN CARVING

Few tools are needed for carving pumpkins, but they are important. A poking tool is used for transferring patterns, a pumpkin drill is used for making holes (such as eyes), and a saw tool is used for the actual carving. A large, sharp knife is needed to cut an opening in the pumpkin and a scraping tool makes cleaning out the pumpkin cavity easier.

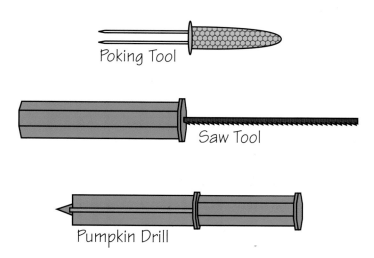

Poking Tool

Saw Tool

Pumpkin Drill

TRANSFERRING PATTERNS ONTO PUMPKINS

The pattern must first be adapted to a size that will work with the size of pumpkin being used. A photo copy, enlarged or reduced appropriately, is the easiest way to assure the design will be in proportion to the size of the pumpkin.

Transferring the pattern onto the pumpkin can be done by first aligning the design in the proper position on the surface of the pumpkin. To allow the pattern to lie snugly on the round surface of the pumpkin, make cuts from the corners of the pattern toward the center and tape it into position.

The pattern can also be pinned to the pumpkin's surface, but in order to avoid unnecessary holes on the surface, it is recommended that the pins be placed in the center of the pattern or in the grooves on the pumpkin.

Once the pattern is in position, carefully punch holes along the outside of the pattern using a poking tool. Do not attempt to poke all the way through the pumpkin, but rather just puncture the surface. For simpler designs, place the holes approximately $1/16$" to $1/8$" apart. If the designs are more intricate, the holes should be placed closer together. Once all the lines have been transferred, remove the pattern. If the "punched pattern" cannot easily be seen, dust the dots with flour.

DRILLING HOLES & CARVING

Before carving the design, drill holes as necessary for eyes and other small, round details using a pumpkin drill. Drilling requires pressure to be applied to the pumpkin, therefore it must be done prior to carving. If not, the drilling process could break the design in areas that have been weakened by carving.

To carve the design, use a saw tool to gently, but firmly, puncture the surface of the pumpkin. Once the saw tool has been inserted straight into the pumpkin, begin to saw from "dot to dot" at a 90° angle.

Start carving from the center of the design and work outward. Do not twist or bend the saw tool as the blade could break.

The trick to perfect carving is not being in a hurry. Once the carving is complete and all pieces are completely cut loose, use the eraser end of a pencil to gently push the carved pieces out.

If a mistake should happen, try pinning the piece back in place using toothpicks or pins.

DISPLAYING THE CARVED MASTERPIECE

Rub vegetable oil or petroleum jelly onto freshly cut areas of the pumpkin to help delay aging. If possible, carve the pumpkin the day before it is to be displayed. Place a candle inside, near the rear of the pumpkin on top of a piece of aluminum foil. When the candle is in position, carefully light it.

Cut a 1"-diameter hole in the top of the pumpkin over the candle to act as a chimney. This allows the air to circulate around the candle and will also prevent the candle from producing excess smoke. Pumpkins with smoke chimneys last longer because the heat can escape. Those that do not have chimneys will actually begin to bake from the inside out.

If no lid was cut out and the opening is in the bottom of the pumpkin, mount a candle on a cut piece of pumpkin or place one in a household candleholder or on a metal jar lid. Light the candle and then place the pumpkin over it.

If living in a climate that gets extremely cold (near freezing) at night or warmer than 60°F in the day, bring the pumpkin inside to prolong its enjoyability!

GENERAL INSTRUCTIONS FOR PUMPKIN EMBELLISHING

Pumpkin embellishing adds interest to any painted or carved pumpkin. In many cases, embellishing is the final, finishing touch that brings the creation to life. Keep in mind that embellishments can also be used on pumpkins that have not been painted or carved!

ADHESIVES USED FOR EMBELLISHING

Many types of adhesives can be used to adhere embellishments to pumpkins: glue gun and glue sticks, craft glue, and industrial-strength glue.

Hot glue is the most common adhesive used within this book, however, it can be substituted with other types of adhesive. If a pumpkin is going to be displayed out of doors where the temperature is cold, hot glue is not recommended and should be substituted with an industrial-strength glue. However, if a pumpkin is going to be displayed indoors, hot glue is a good choice.

Plastic pumpkins are manufactured with different types of plastic and in varying thicknesses. Because of this, it is recommended that hot glue not be used on plastic pumpkins. The plastic could possibly melt from the heat of the glue.

If a pumpkin has been sprayed with a product that doesn't allow adhesives to adhere properly, straight pins can be used to secure the embellishments in place.

MATERIALS USED FOR HAIR

Most pumpkins are painted or carved with a "face" and therefore lend themselves to a hair style that helps add personality and character.

Hair can be made from actual wigs and wiglets, doll hair, curly yarn, fake fur, crinkled paper-grass, fabric strips, curling ribbon, straw, wire, and polyester stuffing.

All of these choices are available in several different colors. Polyester stuffing can be spray-painted with any color!

USING CRAFT FOAM

Craft foam is available in many different colors and is a great medium for embellishing purposes. It can be cut into any shape and can easily be glued to pumpkins. If the craft foam shapes are not as secure as they need to be, straight pins can be used to help secure the pieces in place. Craft foam can be highlighted with acrylic paints. Refer to pages 15, 21, 37, and 42.

MAKING EARS AND ANTENNAE

Oftentimes, pumpkin creatures will need to be embellished with ears or antennae. Antennae can easily be made using wire or pipe cleaners and styrofoam balls or beads. Refer to pages 15, 37, and 47.

The easiest way to make ears is to cut felt fabric into triangles and simply hot-glue them into place on top of the pumpkin. Refer to pages 17 and 19.

Ears can also be made by using wire bent into any shape and size. The wire can be left uncovered or can be covered with any type of fabric by cutting the fabric to size and gluing it to the fronts and backs of the shaped wire ears. Poke the wire ends into the top of the pumpkin and shape as desired. Refer to pages 28, 33, 41, and 42.

GALLERY OF PHOTOS, PATTERNS & INSTRUCTIONS

Refer to page 56

SKELETON SKULL *Refer to page 57*

ANGRY MUMMY *Refer to page 57*

WART WITCH *Refer to page 58*

JAWS *Refer to page 58*

Refer to page 59

SPIDER FAMILY Refer to page 61

WEB OF LIFE Refer to page 61

BROOM HILDA Refer to page 62

MATILDA Refer to page 62

ALLEY CAT
Refer to page 65

SCAR FACE
Refer to page 65

GRIM REAPER
Refer to page 66

CRESCENT MOON
Refer to page 66

CIRCUS CLOWN
Refer to page 69

SPARKLE-EYES
Refer to page 69

OH MY GOSH!
Refer to page 70

FOREVER FRIENDS
Refer to page 70

GARGOYLE

Refer to page 73

PIRATE

Refer to page 73

DEVIL

Refer to page 74

FANCY FACE

Refer to page 74

Refer to page 75

BOOK WORM

Refer to page 77

GOBBLING GOURD Refer to page 77

SAM SCARECROW Refer to page 78

FAT LADY

Refer to page 89

MAD SCIENTIST

Refer to page 89

BRIDE OF FRANKENSTEIN

Refer to page 90

TONGUE-LASHING CLOWN

Refer to page 90

FRANK N. STEIN & WITCH HAZEL

Pictured on page 14

Pumpkin for witch must have a stem!

Acrylic Paints:
Black, gray, green, moss green, sea foam green, red, and white

Embellishment Materials:
Glue gun and glue sticks
Felt witch hat

Painting:
Paint and detail pumpkins, referring to patterns.

Embellishing:
Carefully remove stem from top of witch pumpkin. Hot-glue it to front of pumpkin for a nose, referring to pattern for placement, and hot-glue witch hat to top of pumpkin.

TOAD PRINCE

Pictured on page 15

Acrylic Paints:
Black, bright lime green, dk. green, lt. apple green, metallic gold, bright red, white, and yellow-gold

Embellishment Materials:
Craft glue
Drawing paper

Painting:
Paint and detail pumpkin, referring to pattern.

Embellishing:
Cut a crown from drawing paper. Make sure to allow enough length. Paint both sides with metallic gold. Glue ends of crown together, matching points on crown. Glue crown to top of pumpkin.

GOOGLE-EYED GOURD

Pictured on page 15

Acrylic Paints:
Black, lt. apple green, and very dk. sea foam green

Embellishment Materials:
Glue gun and glue sticks
Pipe cleaners, green: 2
Styrofoam balls, 1½": 2
Square of craft foam: dark sea foam green

Embellishing:
Insert pipe cleaners in top of gourd. Insert the other end of pipe cleaners into styrofoam balls for eyes. Position pipe cleaners, referring to photo. Enlarge patterns as desired and cut nose, hands, and feet from craft foam. Hot-glue in place, referring to photo for placement. Pinch nose to shape it.

Painting:
Paint eyes on styrofoam balls, then paint and detail gourd, referring to pattern.

SIDE-VIEW WITCH

Pictured on page 16

Acrylic Paints:
Black, apple green,
lt. sea foam green, tan,
and off-white

Embellishment Materials:
Glue gun and glue sticks
Curly yarn, black
Witch hat

Painting:
Paint and detail pumpkin,
referring to pattern.

Embellishing:
Cut yarn in varying lengths
and hot-glue it to top of
pumpkin for hair. Hot-glue
witch hat to top of pumpkin.

WRAPPED MUMMY

Pictured on page 16

Acrylic Paints:
Black, red, and white

Embellishment Materials:
Glue gun and glue sticks
Fabric strips, cotton: white

Painting:
Paint and detail pumpkin,
referring to pattern.

Embellishing:
Wrap fabric strips around
pumpkin, mummy-style. Hot-
glue ends to fabric or pumpkin
wherever fabric strips end.

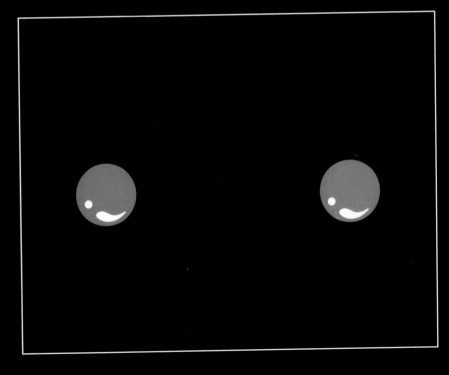

LITTLE DEVIL

Pictured on page 16

Acrylic Paints:
Black,
brick red,
orange-red,
and white

Painting:
Paint pumpkin,
referring
to pattern.

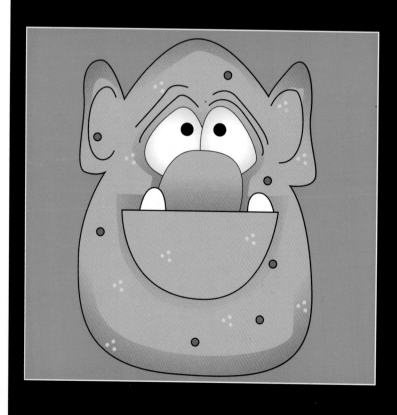

FUZZY FRANKENSTEIN

Pictured on page 16

Acrylic Paints:
Black, pastel blue, lt. green,
lt. lime green, white, and
bright yellow

Embellishment Materials:
Glue gun and glue sticks
Fake fur, yellow

Painting:
Paint and detail pumpkin, referring
to pattern.

Embellishing:
Hot-glue fake fur to top of pumpkin
for hair.

WEREWOLF

Pictured on page 17

Acrylic Paints:
Black, terra cotta brown, gray, taupe, lt. taupe, and white

Embellishment Materials:
Glue gun and glue sticks
Felt fabric, 2" triangles: brown (2)

Painting:
Paint and detail pumpkin, referring to pattern.

Embellishing:
Carefully remove stem from top of pumpkin. Hot-glue felt fabric triangles to top of pumpkin for ears, referring to photo for placement.

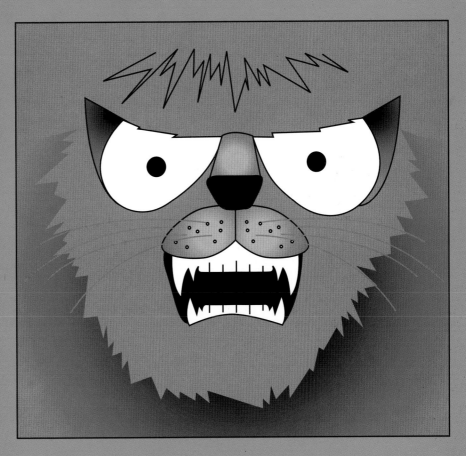

FIRE FACE

Pictured on page 18

Acrylic Paints:
Black, bright blue, dk. blue, pastel blue, sky blue, cream, orange, orchid, plum, red, and yellow

Painting:
Paint and detail pumpkin, referring to pattern. Do not base-coat pumpkin — begin by painting eyebrows, blending red into orange and orange into yellow to give the effect of fire. Paint remaining features. Last, paint unpainted areas of pumpkin with dk. blue.

NINE LIVES

Pictured on page 19

Pumpkin must have a stem!

Acrylic Paints:
Black, gray, dk. green, dk. rose, white, and yellow-gold

Embellishment Materials:
Glue gun and glue sticks
Felt fabric,
   2" triangles: black (2)

Painting:
Paint and detail pumpkin, referring to pattern. Paint pumpkin stem black for nose.

Embellishing:
Hot-glue felt fabric triangles to top of pumpkin for ears, referring to photo for placement.

ALL PUCKERED UP

Pictured on page 20

Pumpkin must have a stem!

Acrylic Paints:
Black, dk. brown, gray, green, dk. green, dk. rose, lt. rose, and white

Embellishment Materials:
Glue gun and glue sticks
Witch hat
Silk flowers, large: 3 or 4

Painting:
Paint and detail pumpkin, referring to pattern. Sponge pumpkin stem with dk. green for nose.

Embellishing:
Hot-glue silk flowers to witch hat, as desired. Hot-glue witch hat at an angle to top of pumpkin.

SKELETON SKULL

Pictured on page 21

Acrylic Paints:
   Black and white

Painting:
Paint and detail pumpkin, referring to pattern.

ANGRY MUMMY

Pictured on page 21

Acrylic Paints:
   Black,
   lt. gray,
   very lt. gray,
   red, and white

Painting:
Paint and detail pumpkin, referring to pattern.

WART WITCH

Pictured on page 21

Acrylic Paints:
Black, coral, lime green, off-white, peach, bright red, and white

Embellishment Materials:
Craft glue
Plastic rhinestones: green (2)
Crinkled paper grass: green

Painting:
Paint and detail pumpkin, referring to pattern.

Embellishing:
Glue plastic rhinestones to front of pumpkin for eyes, referring to pattern for placement. Glue paper grass to top of pumpkin near and around stem for hair.

JAWS

Pictured on page 21

Acrylic Paints:
Black, dk. peach, very lt. peach, purple, red, and white

Embellishment Materials:
Glue gun and glue sticks
Square of craft foam: purple

Painting:
Paint and detail pumpkin, referring to pattern.

Embellishing:
Enlarge patterns as desired and cut fins and tail from craft foam. Hot-glue in place, referring to photo for placement.

BEACH BUM

Pictured on page 22

Acrylic Paints:
Black, baby blue, dk. blue-gray, red, and white

Embellishment Materials:
Glue gun and glue sticks
Plastic sun visor

Painting:
Paint and detail pumpkin, referring to pattern.

Embellishing:
Hot-glue sides of sun visor to top of pumpkin, referring to photo for placement.

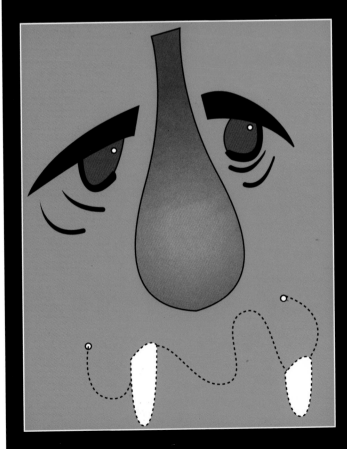

BAD HAIR DAY

Pictured on page 23

Acrylic Paints:
Black, gray, lt. gray, dk. olive green, very lt. olive green, brick red, and white

Embellishment Materials:
Wire, 16-gauge: $2\frac{1}{2}$ yds.
Wire cutters
Sculpting clay, white: 1 pkg.

Painting:
Paint and detail pumpkin, referring to pattern.

Embellishing:
Cut an 8" piece of wire. Twist to form mouth and push sides into pumpkin. Form two pointed teeth from sculpting clay around the wire. Bake according to manufacturer's directions. When cool, dry-brush teeth with gray and lt. gray. Cut seven more pieces of wire in different lengths. Twist and push into top of pumpkin for hair.

WISE OLD OWL

Pictured on page 24

Acrylic Paints:

Black, dk. brown, lt. cocoa brown, dk. gold, lt. gold, gray, very lt. gray, lt. tan, white, and yellow-gold

Painting:

Paint and detail pumpkin, referring to pattern. Use an outward flipping motion to create feathers.

SPIDER FAMILY

Pictured on page 25

Acrylic Paints:
> Black and white

Embellishment Materials:
> Glue gun and glue sticks
> Paper twist, black:
> > 5 ft. for small spider / 10 ft. for large spider
>
> Wire, 24-gauge:
> > 7 ft. for small spider / 12 ft. for large spider

Painting:

Paint and detail pumpkins, referring to pattern.

Embellishing:

Cut eight 6" pieces of paper twist and eight 7" pieces of wire for small spider legs. Cut eight 15" pieces of paper twist and eight 17" pieces of wire for large spider legs. Untwist paper twist and scrunch it around the wires, leaving excess wire extending from one end of each wire. Secure ends of paper twist around wires with hot glue. Hot-glue at several places along edges. Push wire end of each leg into the top sides of pumpkin — four on each side. Bend and shape legs, as desired.

WEB OF LIFE

Pictured on page 25

Acrylic Paint:
> Black

Embellishment Materials:
> Craft glue
> Black spider, 5"
> Prepainted bugs, small: 1 pkg.
> Wire, 16-gauge: 1/2 yd.

Painting:

Paint and detail pumpkin, referring to pattern.

Embellishing:

Bend wire, as desired, and push it into top of black spider. Glue in place. Push other end of wire into top of pumpkin. Glue bugs on spider web.

BROOM HILDA

Pictured on page 25

Acrylic Paints:

Black, dk. brown, dk. green, olive green, very lt. olive green, gold, plum, rose, and white

Embellishment Materials:

Fabric, bright green: 1 yd.
Stringed sequins, green: 5 yds.
Witch hat
Thread, black

Painting:

Paint and detail pumpkin, referring to pattern.

Embellishing:

Measure around opening of witch hat. Cut a 2"-wide strip of fabric that length. Cut remaining fabric in 1"- to 1½"-wide strips in uneven lengths. Lay these strips on top of 2"-wide strip and sew on. Mix in strips of sequins and sew on. Hand-sew 2"-wide strip to inside edge of witch hat. Put hat on top of pumpkin and trim fabric bangs.

MATILDA

Pictured on page 25

Acrylic Paints:

Black, dk. sky blue, very lt. cranberry, fuschia, mauve, peach, and white

Embellishment Materials:

Glue gun and glue sticks
Curly doll hair, brunette
Witch hat

Painting:

Paint and detail pumpkin, referring to pattern.

Embellishing:

Hot-glue doll hair to top of pumpkin. Hot-glue witch hat on top of pumpkin over doll hair.

SIMPLE SUNFLOWER & BEARY-SCARY BEAR

Pictured on page 26

Acrylic Paints:
   Black, brown, gray, green,
   apple green, lt. khaki green,
   white, and yellow-gold

Embellishment Materials:
   Ribbon(s)

Painting:
Paint and detail pumpkins,
referring to patterns.

Embellishing:
Tie a ribbon(s) around stem
of pumpkin.

HAT-SOME TRIO

Pictured on page 27

Acrylic Paints:
Black, dk. mauve, and white

Embellishment Materials:
Glue gun and glue sticks
Straw hats: 3
Ribbon bows: 3
Spanish moss
Silk or plastic greenery with berries
Feathers

Painting:
Paint and detail pumpkins, referring to patterns.

Embellishing:
Hot-glue a straw hat to the top of each pumpkin. Add Spanish moss, greenery, and feathers. Hot-glue a bow to each straw hat, as desired.

ALLEY CAT

Pictured on page 28

Acrylic Paints:
  Black, lt. blue-gray, white, and yellow-gold

Embellishment Materials:
  Wire, 16-gauge
  Wire cutters

Painting:
Paint and detail pumpkin, referring to pattern.

Embellishing:
Cut six 6" pieces of wire. Curl wire to form whiskers. Push three into each side of pumpkin. Carefully remove stem from top of pumpkin. Make ears by referring to instructions on page 12 for making ears out of wire.

SCAR FACE

Pictured on page 28

Acrylic Paints:
  Black,
  lt. blue-gray,
  olive green,
  and white

Painting:
Paint and detail pumpkin, referring to pattern. To get paint to "drip," dilute it to the consistency of watercolor paint. Allow paint to drip down pumpkin, referring to photo.

GRIM REAPER

Pictured on page 28

Acrylic Paints:
Black and orange

Painting:
Paint and detail pumpkin, referring to pattern. Base-coat entire pumpkin with black. When dry, paint the grim reaper with orange. Apply as many coats of orange as necessary to completely cover the black base coat.

CRESCENT MOON

Pictured on page 28

Acrylic Paints:
Lt. turquoise

Painting:
Paint pumpkin, referring to pattern. The actual pattern will not be painted, but rather the remaining surface of the pumpkin. This creates a silhouette effect.

COUNTRY ROAD

Pictured on page 39

Acrylic Paints:
Black, very dk. brown, cocoa brown, lt. cocoa brown, cranberry, very lt. cranberry, fuschia, gold, dk. green, moss green, sea foam green, off-white, purple, and dk. purple

Embellishment Materials:
Glue gun and glue sticks
Silk fall leaves
Scarecrow figure

Painting:
Paint and detail pumpkin, referring to pattern.

Embellishing:
Hot-glue silk leaves and scarecrow to top of pumpkin.

BERRIES

Pictured on page 39

Acrylic Paints:
Black, copper, blue-gray, very dk. gray, lt. olive green, brick red, lt. turquoise, and off-white

Embellishment Materials:
Glue gun and glue sticks
Silk fall leaves
Plastic grapes

Painting:
Paint pumpkin, referring to pattern.

Embellishing:
Hot-glue silk leaves and plastic grapes to top of pumpkin.

PATCHWORK PUMPKIN

Pictured on page 40

Acrylic Paints:

Black, blue, lt. burgundy, gray, dk. green, dk. sea foam green, orange, purple, white, and yellow

Embellishment Materials:

Glue gun and glue sticks
Craft glue
Doily, ecru: 8"
Measuring tape, yellow
Pin cushion, red
Wooden thread spools:
2½" (1), 1⅛" (5), ¾" (3)
Thimbles, silver: 2
Brass scissors charm, 2½"
Embroidery floss
in assorted colors
Buttons, assortment
Pins, assortment
Plastic mice:
1½" (2)
Antiquing gel, brown
Gloss spray sealer

Painting:

Paint and detail pumpkin, referring to pattern.

Embellishing:

Carefully remove stem from top of pumpkin. Apply a thin layer of craft glue to back of doily. Centering, press on top of pumpkin. Allow to dry thoroughly. Antique tape measure, thread spools, thimbles, and scissors charm with antiquing gel. Allow to dry thoroughly. Tie a loopy bow in center of tape measure leaving two 25" tails. Wrap thread spools with assorted colors of embroidery floss leaving 5" to 6" tails. Hot-glue largest spool, pin cushion, and tape measure bow to top of doily, referring to photo for placement. Stack and hot-glue on remaining thread spools, thimbles, buttons, scissors charm, and mice. Loop thread and bow tails and secure with hot glue. Stick pins in pin cushion and in thread spools, as desired.

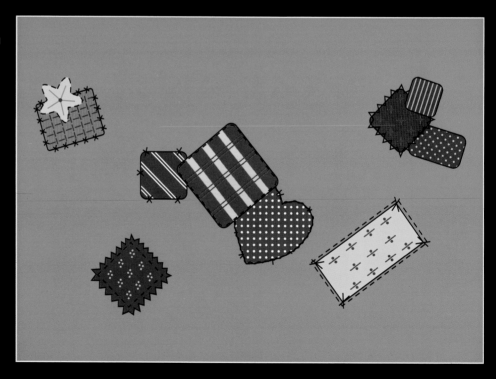

NICE DOGGY
Pictured on page 41

Acrylic Paints:
Black, dk. gold, olive green, dk. peach, bright red, and off-white

Embellishment Materials:
Glue gun and glue sticks
Felt fabric, mustard
Wire, 16-gauge: gold
Wire cutters

Painting:
Paint and detail pumpkin, referring to pattern.

Embellishing:
Cut six 6" pieces of wire. Curl wire to form whiskers. Push three into each side of pumpkin. Make ears by referring to instructions on page 12 for making ears out of wire and covering them with fabric. Highlight ears with acrylic paints.

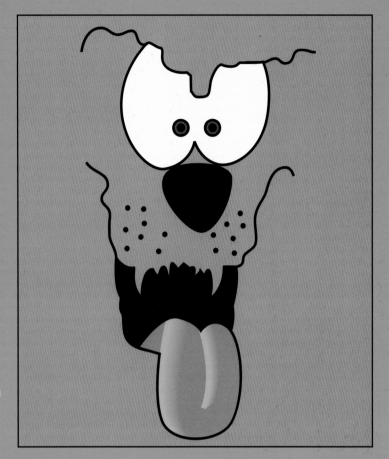

COUNTRY CROW
Pictured on page 41

Acrylic Paints:
Black, mustard, rust, dk. taupe, and white

Embellishment Materials:
Glue gun and glue sticks
Straw hat, 6" diameter

Painting:
Paint and detail pumpkin, referring to pattern.

Embellishing:
Hot-glue straw hat to top of pumpkin.

BEARY
SPECIAL BEAR

Pictured on page 41

Acrylic Paints:
Black, very lt. mauve, lt. tan, dk. taupe, and white

Embellishment Materials:
Glue gun and glue sticks
Strip of blue-print cotton fabric

Painting:
Paint and detail pumpkin, referring to pattern.

Embellishing:
Tie fabric strip into a bow with long tails. Hot-glue bow to top of pumpkin and tails to sides of pumpkin for a hair bow.

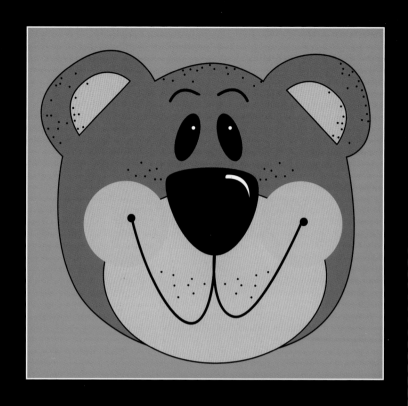

FRIGHTENED
CAT

Pictured on page 41

Acrylic Paints:
Black, copper, and dk. gold

Embellishment Materials:
Glue gun and glue sticks
Wired silk leaves

Painting:
Paint and detail pumpkin, referring to pattern.

Embellishing:
Hot-glue silk leaves to top of pumpkin.

JACK-O-RABBIT

Pictured on page 42

Acrylic Paints:

Black, lt. brown, lt. gray, green, lt. green, pink, lt. tan, very dk. taupe, and off-white

Embellishment Materials:

Glue gun and glue sticks
Wire, 20-gauge: 1 yd.
Wire cutters
Craft foam: gray

Painting:

Paint and detail pumpkin, referring to pattern. Paint highlights on rabbit ears.

Embellishing:

Enlarge patterns as desired and cut ears from craft foam. Cut two 8" pieces of wire. Hot-glue wire along center back of each ear leaving at least 1" extending at lower ends. Press ears together at the bottom, around wire, to form a tuck in craft foam. Push wires into top of pumpkin and bend ears, as desired. Cut four more pieces of wire in 5" lengths. Twist and push into front of pumpkin for whiskers.

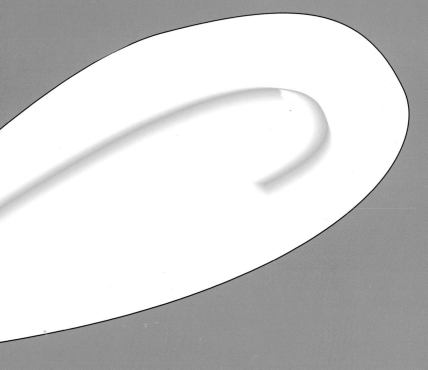

HAPPY HOBOS

Pictured on page 43

Acrylic Paints:
Black, gray, red, light rust, and white

Embellishment Materials:
Glue gun and glue sticks
Assorted hats: 3
Silk scarf

Painting:
Paint and detail pumpkins, referring to patterns.

Embellishing:
Tie silk scarf into a bow. Hot-glue scarf and hats onto tops of pumpkins.

MOON EYES

Pictured on page 44

Acrylic Paints:
Black,
dk. blue-gray,
navy blue,
dk. gold,
yellow-gold, and
sparkle glaze

Painting:
Paint and detail
pumpkin, referring
to pattern. Paint
over eyes with
sparkle glaze.

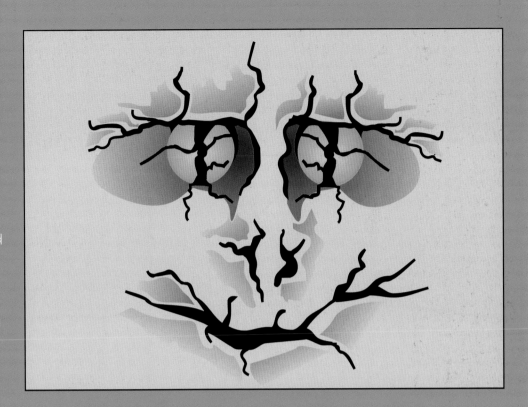

FULL MOON

Pictured on page 44

Acrylic Paints:
Black and
bright yellow

Painting:
Paint and detail
pumpkin, referring
to pattern.

PUMPKIN COACH

Pictured on page 45

Acrylic Paints:

Black, metallic gold,
silver-gray, and white

Materials to Assemble Stand:

Wooden plaque, oval: 6⅝" x 5"
Wooden spoked wheels: 2½" (4)
Wooden pegs for axles: 2" (4)
Drill and drill bit, 5/16"
Wood glue
Gloss spray sealer

Painting:

Paint and detail pumpkin, referring to
pattern. Paint oval plaque and center and
outer areas of wheels with white. Paint
spokes, pegs, and routed edge of oval plaque
with metallic gold. Spray with spray sealer.

Assembling Stand:

Refer to photo to mark placement for wheels
on oval plaque. Drill holes. Slide one peg
through each wheel and glue into drilled holes.
Allow to dry thoroughly.

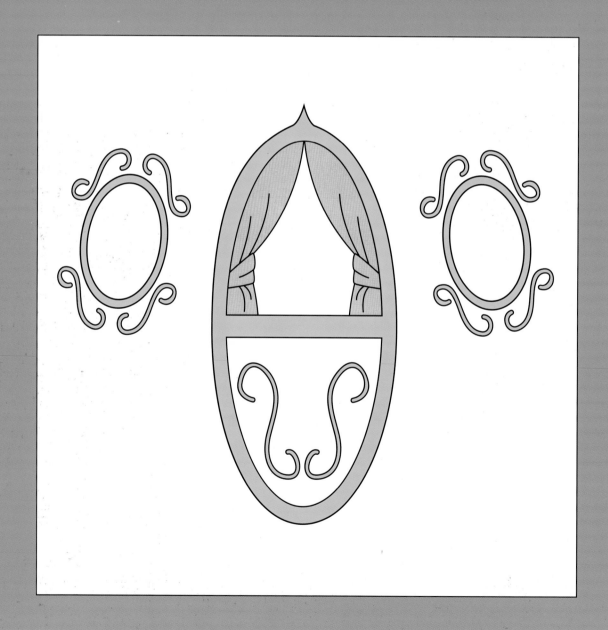

FAT LADY

Pictured on page 46

Acrylic Paints:

Black, robin egg blue, lt. robin egg blue, teal green, lt. teal green, peach, lt. pink, red, and white

Embellishment Materials:

Curly wig, white
Hoop post earrings, large
Straight pins

Painting:

Paint and detail pumpkin, referring to pattern.

Embellishing:

Pin wig to top of pumpkin. Push post earrings into sides of pumpkin.

MAD SCIENTIST

Pictured on page 46

Acrylic Paints:

Black, cranberry, very lt. gold, bright green, very lt. peach, and white

Embellishment Materials:

Wiglets, white: 2
Straight pins

Painting:

Paint and detail pumpkin, referring to pattern.

Embellishing:

Pin wig to sides of pumpkin.

89

BRIDE OF FRANKENSTEIN

Pictured on page 46

Acrylic Paints:
Black, cranberry, gray,
dk. green, lt. shade of
dk. green, and white

Embellishment Materials:
Glue gun and glue sticks
Stuffing, polyester
Spray paint, black

Painting:
Paint and detail pumpkin,
referring to pattern.
Sponge paint background.
Spray paint polyester stuffing.

Embellishing:
Hot-glue stuffing to top of pumpkin.

TONGUE-LASHING CLOWN

Pictured on page 46

Acrylic Paints:
Black, bone,
dk. orchid,
and purple

Embellishment Materials:
Clown wig, multi-colored
Straight pins

Painting:
Paint and detail pumpkin,
referring to pattern.
Sponge paint background.

Embellishing:
Pin wig to top of pumpkin.

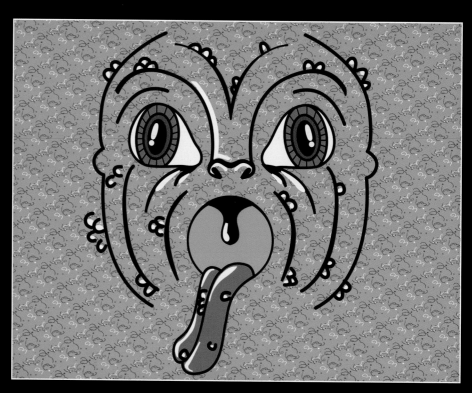

INSECT

Pictured on page 47

Acrylic Paints:

Black, very dk. brown, bright lime green, very dk. brown, very dk. sea foam green, and very dk. taupe

Embellishment Materials:

Glue gun and glue sticks
Wire, 16-gauge: 24"
Wire cutters
Small wooden beads, green: 2

Painting:

Paint and detail pumpkin, referring to pattern.

Embellishing:

Cut two 12" pieces of wire. Curl wire to form antennae. Hot-glue a bead to the end of each antennae. Push the antennae into top of pumpkin and position, as desired.

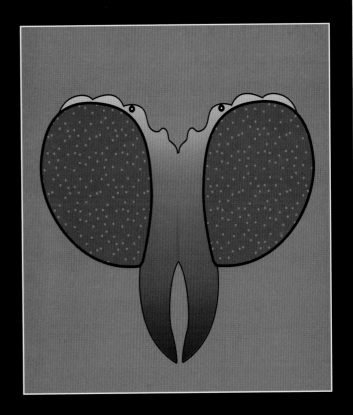

ALIEN

Pictured on page 47

Acrylic Paints:

Black, very lt. gold, lt. gray, olive green, lt. teal green, very lt. mustard, and dk. brick red

Embellishment Materials:

Pipe cleaners, white: 2
Styrofoam balls, 1¹/₂": 2

Painting:

Paint and detail pumpkins, referring to patterns. Paint styrofoam balls.

Embellishing:

Push a styrofoam ball into the end of each pipe cleaner for antennae. Push the opposite end of each pipe cleaner into top of pumpkin and position, as desired.

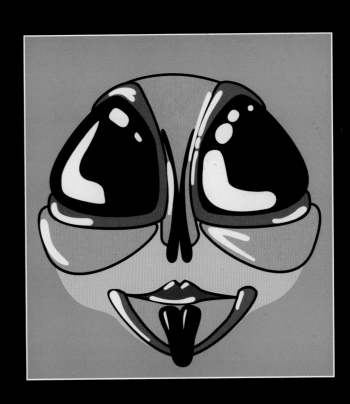

MINI PUMPKINS

Pictured on page 48

Acrylic Paints:

Black, dk. gray, bright green, orange, dk. orchid, orange-red, white, and yellow-gold

Painting:

Paint and detail pumpkins, referring to patterns.

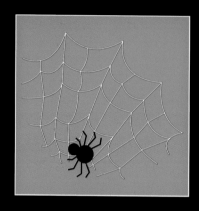

PUMPKIN TOPIARY TREE

Pictured on page 49

Acrylic Paints:
Dk. brown, gold, and orange

Materials to Assemble Tree:
Papier-mâché pumpkin,
   4$\frac{1}{2}$" diameter
Silk leaf vine
Wooden dowel,
   11" long x $\frac{3}{4}$" diameter
Clay pot, 6" diameter
Floral tape, brown
Craft knife
Glue gun and glue sticks
Sculpting clay
Plaster of Paris
Florist's foam
Spanish moss
Flower picks in fall colors

Painting and Assembling:
Paint clay pot with dk. brown and wrap dowel with brown floral tape. Make a hole in bottom of pumpkin with craft knife. Push dowel into hole and hot-glue in place. Seal hole in bottom of clay pot with small piece of sculpting clay. Mix plaster according to manufacturer's directions and pour into clay pot. (If the clay pot was completely filled with plaster all at once, the pot would break because of the heat of the plaster.) Place dowel in clay pot, centering, and secure so it cannot shift. Allow to set up. Continue process until clay pot is full, leaving enough room to add florist's foam. Dry-brush grooves in pumpkin and wrapped dowel with dk. brown. Dry-brush both sides of vine with dk. brown, gold, and orange. Poke holes in top of pumpkin and insert vines and hot-glue in place. Add florist's foam to inside top of clay pot and cover with Spanish moss. Add flower picks that coordinate with fall colors.

MINIATURE PUMPKINS

Pictured on page 49

Acrylic Paints:
Black, bright blue, brick red, and white

Painting:
Paint and detail pumpkins, referring to patterns.

TOLE PUMPKIN

Pictured on page 50

Acrylic Paints:
Black, bright green, peach, rose, and white

Building Materials, Tools & Embellishments:
Pine, $\frac{1}{2}$" or $\frac{3}{4}$"
Saw
Sandpaper
Wood sealer
Wood glue
Wire, 16-gauge
Wire cutters
Curly doll hair, auburn

Preparing Wood:
Make a photo copy of pattern pieces provided, reducing or enlarging as desired. Trace pattern onto pine and cut out. Sand until rough edges are smooth.
Seal wood with wood sealer according to manufacturer's directions. Allow to dry thoroughly. Place wood pieces together to make sure they fit nicely. Take pieces apart.

Painting:
Base-coat one side and all edges of each pumpkin piece with two to three coats of acrylic paint. Allow to dry thoroughly. Base-coat remaining side of pumpkin pieces with the same number of coats, and let dry. Paint and detail both sides, referring to patterns. When thoroughly dry, place pieces together and secure with a small amount of wood glue.

Embellishing:
Use wire to form eye glasses. Glue glasses to pumpkin's nose and glue doll hair to top of pumpkin.

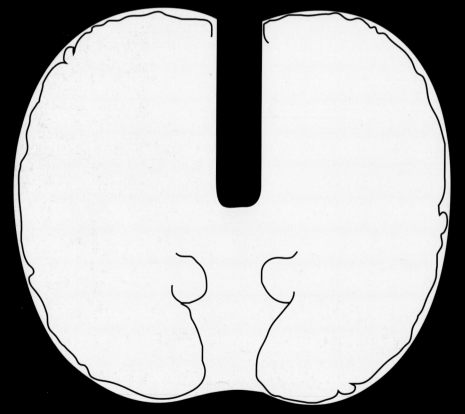

94

METRIC CONVERSIONS

INCHES TO MILLIMETRES AND CENTIMETRES

MM-Millimetres   CM-Centimetres

INCHES	MM	CM	INCHES	CM	INCHES	CM
1/8	3	0.9	9	22.9	30	76.2
1/4	6	0.6	10	25.4	31	78.7
3/8	10	1.0	11	27.9	32	81.3
1/2	13	1.3	12	30.5	33	83.8
5/8	16	1.6	13	33.0	34	86.4
3/4	19	1.9	14	35.6	35	88.9
7/8	22	2.2	15	38.1	36	91.4
1	25	2.5	16	40.6	37	94.0
1 1/4	32	3.2	17	43.2	38	96.5
1 1/2	38	3.8	18	45.7	39	99.1
1 3/4	44	4.4	19	48.3	40	101.6
2	51	5.1	20	50.8	41	104.1
2 1/2	64	6.4	21	53.3	42	106.7
3	76	7.6	22	55.9	43	109.2
3 1/2	89	8.9	23	58.4	44	111.8
4	102	10.2	24	61.0	45	114.3
4 1/2	114	11.4	25	63.5	46	116.8
5	127	12.7	26	66.0	47	119.4
6	152	15.2	27	68.6	48	121.9
7	178	17.8	28	71.1	49	124.5
8	203	20.3	29	73.7	50	127.0

YARDS TO METRES

YARDS	METRES	YARDS	METRES	YARDS	METRES	YARDS	METRES	YARDS	METRES
1/8	0.11	2 1/8	1.94	4 1/8	3.77	6 1/8	5.60	8 1/8	7.43
1/4	0.23	2 1/4	2.06	4 1/4	3.89	6 1/4	5.72	8 1/4	7.54
3/8	0.34	2 3/8	2.17	4 3/8	4.00	6 3/8	5.83	8 3/8	7.66
1/2	0.46	2 1/2	2.29	4 1/2	4.11	6 1/2	5.94	8 1/2	7.77
5/8	0.57	2 5/8	2.40	4 5/8	4.23	6 5/8	6.06	8 5/8	7.89
3/4	0.69	2 3/4	2.51	4 3/4	4.34	6 3/4	6.17	8 3/4	8.00
7/8	0.80	2 7/8	2.63	4 7/8	4.46	6 7/8	6.29	8 7/8	8.12
1	0.91	3	2.74	5	4.57	7	6.40	9	8.23
1 1/8	1.03	3 1/8	2.86	5 1/8	4.69	7 1/8	6.52	9 1/8	8.34
1 1/4	1.14	3 1/4	2.97	5 1/4	4.80	7 1/4	6.63	9 1/4	8.46
1 3/8	1.26	3 3/8	3.09	5 3/8	4.91	7 3/8	6.74	9 3/8	8.57
1 1/2	1.37	3 1/2	3.20	5 1/2	5.03	7 1/2	6.86	9 1/2	8.69
1 5/8	1.49	3 5/8	3.31	5 5/8	5.14	7 5/8	6.97	9 5/8	8.80
1 3/4	1.60	3 3/4	3.43	5 3/4	5.26	7 3/4	7.09	9 3/4	8.92
1 7/8	1.71	3 7/8	3.54	5 7/8	5.37	7 7/8	7.20	9 7/8	9.03
2	1.83	4	3.66	6	5.49	8	7.32	10	9.14

INDEX

THE REALLY, REALLY, REALLY EASY
STEP-BY-STEP GUIDE TO CREATING & EDITING
DIGITAL VIDEOS
USING YOUR COMPUTER

for absolute beginners of all ages

Christian Darkin
Series created by Gavin Hoole and Cheryl Smith

Contents

Read this before you start

Today camcorders are everywhere and you can record video at varying qualities using a whole range of devices. There's also a growing range of ways to show that video once you've shot it – you can play it through mobile phones, burn it onto DVDs or broadcast it over the Internet.

It's now quite possible to shoot footage comparable to broadcast television on a home camcorder, and for friends on the other side of the world to watch your home movies on their computer screens almost as soon as you've shot them.

Video has become available to everyone as a way to record and communicate, and a quick look around Internet sites like YouTube will reveal that making a video is now as easy and natural to many people as writing a letter.

Where newcomers to video (as well as a fair number who have already mastered the basics) generally struggle is in the process of shaping the raw footage from the huge range of camcorders available into something interesting and watchable, and outputting it in a format that can be watched on TV, a computer or the Internet.

Modern computers can easily handle the challenges of editing video and all Windows PCs come with editing software already installed. All that's needed are the skills to cut and edit along with a little care in shooting your footage in the first place.

And that's what this book will provide. The following chapters will take you through what to look for in choosing a camcorder, and how to approach shooting in a variety of situations.

You'll then look at getting shot footage onto a computer, and cutting it into interesting and professional-looking videos through a series of detailed step-by-step projects. Finally, you'll discover how to take your finished video and upload it to the Internet, burn it onto DVD and even copy it onto an ipod.

 MICROSOFT WINDOWS VISTA HAS BEEN USED FOR THIS BOOK This book assumes that you will have easy access to a computer as well as an Internet connection, and the screenshots and procedures given are based on the Microsoft Windows Vista operating system. If you are using some other operating system you will need to make adaptations accordingly when you work through the step-by-step procedures and refer to the accompanying screenshots.

THE USER-FRIENDLY VISUAL SYSTEM

The same user-friendly visual system as used in all the books in this series makes it really, really, really easy for you to enjoy creating and editing your own digital videos.

Colour-coded text windows are used throughout the book so that you can see at a glance the type of information you're looking at:

- introductions and explanations in normal black text on a white background;

- step-by-step action procedures in yellow boxes;

- hints and tips in blue boxes;

- very important notes and warnings in boxes with red borders;

- supportive explanatory information in grey panels.

Where necessary, the detailed procedures are supported by illustrations to make learning easier.

 WORK YOUR WAY THROUGH EACH CHAPTER IN SEQUENCE This step-by-step workbook is designed to be used chapter-by-chapter. Working through it in its proper sequence will help you do 'first things first' and learn the correct ways of tackling the various processes and methodologies that follow in subsequent chapters. You'll first discover the important factors in choosing a camcorder, and the best ways to shoot video for desktop editing. We'll take a look at some common shooting situations and how to approach them. Then we'll tackle how to get footage onto your computer. After that, we'll get into the process of editing progressing from simple projects through to more advanced techniques. Finally we'll look at how to publish your finished videos to DVD and over the Internet.

Let's have some fun!

1 Camcorders and recording equipment

Finding the right camcorder for you is important but as there are so many to choose from, and new models and styles are appearing every day, we can't tell you which model will suit you, and even if we could, the information would be out of date before it was printed. What we can do is tell you what features to look out for when you buy and what the advantages and disadvantages of different types of camcorder are.

HOW TO CHOOSE A CAMERA

Let's start with a quick tour around a traditional camcorder. Here are some top tips for what to look out for, what's useful and what isn't:

Lens – take a look at the camcorder's lens. That's where the light is coming in, so it needs to be of a reasonable size. If it's the size of a pea, you shouldn't expect great pictures.

Zooms – there are two types of zoom: optical and digital. Digital zooms are available on many camcorders. They're usually completely pointless and not only give you very wobbly shots, but also blur and pixillate your pictures giving an effect that's more like pressing your nose against the TV screen than bringing the subject closer to the camera. Optical zooms can be useful, but bear in mind that the more you zoom in, the shakier the camera will be.

Microphone – most camcorders don't have very good microphones. Try to make sure you get one which is biased towards what's in front of the camera rather than taking sound from all around (including behind the camera).

Also, look for headphone and microphone sockets so that you can monitor sound quality and, if you need to, plug in an extra mic.

Low light shooting – try to check your camera in low light. Can it handle shooting indoors on a dull day? Usually when a camera is struggling with lighting, the picture becomes grainy and the auto focus starts to fail.

Very low light shooting – some camcorders solve the low light problem with an infra-red mode that illuminates everything within a couple of metres of the lens in a ghoulish green light (this light is only visible when looking through the camera's viewfinder and will not show up on the video). Others reduce the frame-rate of the image so shots become jerky and blurred, but remain visible. Neither is a perfect solution, but the infra-red light option is probably the better option.

Shooting controls – pick up the camcorder and your thumb should rest naturally on the record button. Your index finger should be within easy reach of the zoom control. Pick a camcorder that fits well in your hand and you'll be able to take steady shots easily.

Other controls – find out how easy it is to control the camera's other functions – like the light level and the focus. Some camcorders allow you to adjust the manual focus using a button, while others use a ring around the lens or use a touch sensitive viewscreen. Ask yourself if you're really going to want to operate any of these controls while filming.

Picture quality – don't be satisfied with looking at the image in the camera's viewfinder. The viewscreen is only a couple of hundred pixels in size, so you can't possibly tell what kind of picture quality you're getting. The only way to know is to record some footage and then watch it back on a big TV or computer screen (watching "live" footage won't tell you how well the picture is being compressed).

TIP: PICTURE QUALITY

Compare different camcorders using the Internet. Try to get hold of some sample footage or at least still frame grabs (not still photos) from each model and watch them back at full-screen size. This will give you the best idea of the camera's picture quality.

Auto focus and iris – test out the camera by swinging it from a bright area to a dark corner very quickly. How fast does it react? Do the same for close up and distant objects to check the auto focus.

In-camera effects – many cameras have fades, mixes, sepia and other effects you can add to your footage as you record. There's absolutely nothing these effects can do that you can't do more easily and more controllably later on your computer. Be warned that if you do use an effect on the camera and decide you don't like it later, there will be nothing you can do.

Canon XL high end camera

CAMERAS THAT AREN'T CAMERAS

It seems nowadays that everything is a video camera. You can record video on most digital stills cameras, on your computer's webcam and even on your mobile phone.

Most of these devices aren't primarily designed as camcorders. Although they may have the memory, the processing power and even the electronics to produce good video images, the lenses and the microphones on these devices are almost always tiny and not really up to the job of capturing high quality video footage.

If you haven't got anything else to hand, it's quite possible to record usable video with, for example, a stills camera, but when you come to play it back you're likely to find that it suffers from the following problems:

- **Poor quality sound**.
- **Bad lighting** – light levels have to be detected automatically and the lenses aren't perfect so you'll find low light a particular problem, leading to dark images.
- **Blocky pictures** – the video on these devices tends to be highly compressed in order to get as much as possible on a memory card. This means footage can become blocky and jerky, especially when there's a lot of movement in the shot.
- **Low frame rates and resolution** – images tend to be designed for the Web rather than TV, and that means lower quality images and lower frame-rates.

Mustek digital video camera   Fuji stills camera   Fuji stills camera

These machines aren't yet sophisticated enough to be a substitute for a decent camcorder, but if they're all you've got handy you'll still be able to edit their footage on your computer and cut it in just the same way.

RECORDING FORMATS

It used to be that all camcorders recorded their images to tapes. There were a couple of different formats, but they all worked in pretty much the same way. Over the last few years, however, there has been an explosion of different formats and qualities aimed at TV, the Internet, and the new High Definition TV standard.

Here are a few formats you might come across. Within each of these are a few variations, but you needn't worry too much about them unless you're shooting professionally:

Standard Definition (SD) – the standard format for TV. Pictures are 720 x 576 pixels in size in the UK or 720 x 480 in the US. You'll see that quality of video every time you turn on the TV as it's what most TV programmes are currently transmitted on. If you want decent quality videos, you should make sure that whatever machine you buy produces at least this quality of video.

High Definition (HD) – the best quality video you can get. Pictures are shot at anything up to 1920 x 1080 pixels (but most often 1440 x 1080) – which effectively means they're good enough to be shown on a full size cinema screen. In order to play back HD video you need a HD Television (or you can watch them on your computer screen). In order to output them from your computer, you need a special DVD writer (called a blu-ray or HD-DVD writer) and a blu-ray or HD-DVD player to play them. As this technology is new, for the next few years this is likely to remain a bit frustrating, and you're most likely going to end up burning your HD movies onto ordinary standard definition DVDs once you've finish editing them. On a positive note, though, the shots will look great even then and they will still be stored as HD on your computer.

VGA or SVGA – the standards for multimedia and the Internet. Video is recorded at either 320 x 240 or 640 x 480 pixels. It's only non-standard video recorders (like digital stills cameras, mobile phones or memory card camcorders) that record to these standards and they do it to fit more video into their modest memory. You can still use video from these devices in your productions, and sometimes it will look okay – however, if you're buying a device specifically for video, look for a higher recording standard.

Video recorded at 320 x 240 pixels

RECORDING MEDIA

It's now possible to capture your video onto DVD, tape, memory card, hard disk or even straight onto to your computer using a webcam. Here are a few of the recording media you're likely to discover on the high street:

Canon DVD camcorder

DVD

DVD – a double-sided compact disk with a memory roughly equivalent to 24 CDs. You can take the disk straight out of the camcorder and put it into your DVD player to watch your recordings, but editing can be trickier because you need to transfer the footage to an editable format with a special piece of software.

Mini DV tape

Canon DV camcorder

DV tape – a small tape about the size of a matchbox. DV recordings are well up to the quality of TV, and transferring the footage to a computer for editing is well supported by all editing programs. On the downside, you'll need to transfer your tape to your hard drive and it will take the same amount of time as it did to shoot. DV footage takes up a lot of space on your computer too.

HDV – uses identical tapes to a DV camcorder, but shoots in High Definition (HDV camcorders can also shoot DV if you want them to). It's just as easy to transfer to your computer, and takes up the same amount of space. However, because it's bigger, it can slow down editing, especially on an older PC.

HDV camcorder

HDD – Hard Disk Drive. The camcorder contains a miniature hard disk drive (just like the one in your computer) and stores video to this. The quality can be set (depending on the model you buy) to anything from VGA right up to High Definition. The higher the quality of images you record, the less you'll be able to fit on the disk. However, when you've finished recording, you'll usually transfer your footage to your computer for editing anyway so this isn't too much of a problem. The formats HDD cameras shoot in do require a little work before you can edit them comfortably, but you shouldn't buy a hard drive camcorder unless you're planning to use a computer to edit or transfer its footage.

HDD camcorder

Memory card – camcorders (as well as stills cameras, phones, and so on) that write their video to memory cards can be very cheap. They can also be extremely tough because they have no moving parts. They're often very small and so sometimes have poor quality lenses, and not much in the way of image stabilisation, zooms, and other useful functions. You'll need to check that the model you're looking at will record a decent quality of image (at least SD quality). Don't be confused – the still photo quality is not the same as the video recording quality. It's also worth checking the frame-rate of the recording (which needs to be at least 25 frames per second for TV quality pictures).

Recording to memory cards makes transferring footage to your computer a cinch and most editing software will work happily with the video clips recorded.

Canon memory card camcorder

Sony memory card

Choosing a camcorder is a personal decision based on what you intend to use it for, how comfortable you feel holding it, and of course, how much you're willing to spend. If budgets are tight, look for a memory card camcorder or an older DV machine. If you want quality, go for an HD camcorder. If portability is important, look for a hard drive or memory card camera. Finally, if you've got nothing else to hand, use a mobile phone or stills camera – but be prepared for the footage not to look quite as good as it might.

2 Shooting your video

Whatever kind of video you want to make, shooting good footage in the first place is the key. If you have a good range of strong shots to work with, editing and presenting your production is going to be much easier.

And it's not rocket science – in this chapter, we'll take a look at a few basic rules for shooting good video footage. Follow these tips and you can be sure that when you come to fit the various parts of your video together they'll be interesting to watch and make sense.

RECORDING ON A CAMCORDER

Most modern camcorders are pretty easy to work with. All you need do is turn them on and hit the big red record button to start and stop recording. It's as simple as that and with very good automatic focus and lighting level adjustment, you shouldn't need to do anything else to get good footage in normal conditions.

The zoom is usually a rocker button located above the record button allowing you to zoom in or out.

Some more up-market camcorders allow you to zoom using a ring around the lens (which can generally be switched between controlling the focus and the zoom functions). The more you zoom in, the more any movement you make will shake the camera, so the more wobbly your shots will be (see note on page 14 and page 15).

RECORDING ON A STILLS CAMERA

Most stills cameras have different modes accessible from a small thumb wheel around which different icons are arranged. Often you'll find a camcorder icon allowing you to record video. To use it, simply turn the wheel to the icon and use the shutter to start and stop recording.

Cameras differ but many won't let you zoom in while you're filming. Most don't record full TV quality video, but there is often a choice of video resolutions to be found in the camera's setup menu. The higher the resolution, the clearer your videos will be but the more space they'll take up on your memory card.

Big red button

Zoom control

Stills camera control

Look for a setting of at least 640 x 480 if you can. Also, if there's an option for setting the frame-rate, make sure it's at least 25 frames per second or your shots will look jerky.

Video recorded at 640 x 480 pixels

RECORDING ON A MOBILE PHONE

Mobile phones usually have the same restrictions as stills cameras and you'll have to choose a resolution for your video footage. Phone cameras aren't usually of high quality – their lenses are tiny and their memories small. However, you can still record usable video from them. In fact mobile phone footage from eye-witnesses has often been used on news programmes.

Mobile phone video

You won't find a huge range of manual functions here and most don't even have a zoom. This makes recording on a phone very easy – how to start and stop the device is more or less all you have to learn. However, most mobiles won't currently record more than a few minutes of footage before their memory cards are filled, so you'll have to empty them onto your computer regularly and be economical with your shooting.

COMPOSING YOUR SHOT

Follow these pointers for professional-looking video footage:

Stability

Before turning on the camera, make sure you're ready to film. Stand straight in a comfortable posture with your feet apart and both hands keeping the camera steady. Face the action directly and make sure you can perform any movement you want to comfortably and securely.

Filming people

Most of your shots will probably include people. Try to observe these principles in mind when filming human subjects:

Eyes on a third – however you frame your shot, place the eyes of your main subject about a third of the way from the top of the frame. Whether they're in close up or at a distance, this will give the shot a good balance.

Eyes on a third

"Looking room" – if someone is looking to one side of the shot or the other, give them a little "looking room" in the picture. In other words, frame them so there's more of a gap in front of their nose than behind their ear. This looks better because the viewer's attention is drawn in the same direction as the subject's. It also means that if they move forward, you'll be ready to follow them with the camera.

Long shots and close-ups – a long shot shows the whole scene and lets the viewer understand what's happening and where. A close up focuses attention on what someone's doing or saying. Make sure you shoot a good range of close-up and long shots of whatever you're filming.

A shot with "looking room"

Medium close-ups – Medium close-up **(MCU)** is probably the most widely used shot on TV. It's basically the subject's head and shoulders directly in the centre of the screen. There's a little room above the person's head. Their eyes are a third of the way from the top, and the shot finishes in the middle of the chest. You'll see **MCU**s in everything from the news to movies because it's generally thought of as the closest you can get to the view you have when you're having a conversation with someone.

Medium close-up

Filming conversations

When there's more than one person in the shot, things get a little more complicated. Try to get the main speakers in shot, but without leaving a big gap between them in the centre of the screen. This often means moving to one side so that one person is facing the camera and the other is facing away. Avoid the temptation to keep panning the camera back and forth between the speakers all the time.

Conversations

Scenery

Don't just film hours of beautiful scenery in which nothing is happening. By all means get a few establishing shots, but balance them with closer shots which give the viewer something to focus on.

Make sure each shot is "about" something – that you're focusing on a detail you wouldn't take notice of in a wider shot.

Try to get some action in each shot – either by moving the camera (see page 16) or by focusing on something actually happening. A still shot of a green field isn't interesting, but get shots of someone walking through a field, close-ups of cows feeding, flowers moving in the breeze, birds flying overhead or bees pollinating the flowers and you'll have an interesting sequence.

Wildlife

The problem with filming wildlife is that you don't know what it's going to do next. You also usually can't get close, so you'll have to zoom in. The key here is patience and stability. Get hold of a tripod for your camera and be prepared to waste a lot of tape and a lot of time. When your subject finally makes an appearance, you'll need to be ready with your shot lined up and your settings all planned. Resist the urge to zoom right in. If your subject makes a sudden move, you want the shot to be wide enough to give you time to pan with it.

Wildlife filming

Moving shots

Use camera movement with care. It's usually best to keep the camera still if you can, and if you do move, move slowly, smoothly and with purpose. Decide before you move when and where you're going to stop. Keep filming for a few seconds (count slowly to 5) before and after the movement to give yourself time to cut in and out. Practise your move before you record if you can so that you know you'll be able to keep your balance throughout. Stay zoomed out; the more your shot is zoomed in, the more wobbly it will be, making it hard to get smooth movement. Try to get hold of a tripod designed for video (look for tripods boasting a **fluid head**), allowing you to move the camera steadily and film more smoothly.

SHOOTING FOR THE EDIT

The difference between picking up a camcorder ten years ago and doing the same today is editing. Today, you're likely to edit whatever you film in some way before you show it to anyone. You should be thinking about editing before you even start shooting – the following advice will make this second nature.

Overshoot

Tape and DVDs are cheap. Memory cards are getting cheaper. If you're editing you can cut out unwanted footage, but you can't manufacture footage that was never there. If in doubt, roll the camera.

TRADITIONAL CAMERA MOVES

Panning – turning the camera through an angle while keeping it in the same position. Pans are good for landscape shots or to take in a wide scene.

Tilting – again, the camera stays in the same position, but tilts up or down to take in higher or lower parts of the scene.

Tracking - The camera stays at the same angle, but you move with it. Tracking shots are great for following the action, but they can be difficult to execute smoothly.

Hand held – the camera moves freely as you pan, move and tilt to cover the scene. Hand held shots are useful when you don't know what's going to happen next, but you need to be especially careful about holding the camera steady.

Zooming – using the zoom controls to zoom in or out. Most TV programmes use zooms very rarely. This is because it's alien to the way the human eye works, so doesn't look great. It's also because the zoom on most cameras isn't easy to control smoothly. It's best to pick your zoom level before you turn the camera on, and stick with it.

Start and end

Start filming a few seconds early, and stop a few seconds after the action has finished. You might want to fade into or out of the shot or give it a little extra time when you edit, so don't be in a hurry to stop the camera.

Think in sequences not shots

Whatever you're filming, you're telling a story. If it's a wedding, the story is clear – it's the story of the wedding day. But whether you're filming a day out, a birthday party or taking shots on holiday, the aim is still going to be to tell the story of your event.

A story is more than just a collection of shots. You'll need to keep in mind the story you plan to tell, and concentrate your filming on those things that help you tell it.

Make sure you record a range of **long shots** which show the whole scene and tell your audience what is happening and where. Complement these with **close-ups** which show the detail of what is happening. Getting a good range of different looking shots will help you create a great video later on.

Get **cut-aways** too. **Cut-aways** are shots that don't have much to do with the main action, but which can be slotted in anywhere later on to cover gaps in your recording or cuts (see page 52). For example, the reaction of crowds watching a sporting event can be slipped in anywhere during the event if the camera goes out of focus, or you want to cut out a section of the action.

Cut-away shot of the watching crowd

GETTING GOOD SOUND

The quickest way to make your video look more professional is to get better sound. If you have good, sharp audio and can hear everything that's being said, you can get away with a wobbly camera, poor focus and lighting or casual editing. On the other hand, if your sound is muffled or crackly, it doesn't matter how well shot your video is – it will play badly.

Built in microphones

Most of the time, the microphone on your camcorder will not be of great quality. It will be designed to capture sound from all around it – rather than sound coming from whatever's in front of the camera (i.e. what you're trying to film). It will be subject to noise from the camera's motors (its zoom and tape or CD motors) and it will be unable to distinguish, for example, between a person's voice and the traffic noise in the background.

Stills cameras and phones also have microphones, but these are generally even worse. This doesn't mean you can't get a decent performance out of them – you just need to be careful.

TIPS: GETTING GOOD SOUND FROM A BUILT IN MICROPHONE

- Get close. Don't stand a long way away and zoom in; get close to your subject and zoom out.
- Pay attention. Listen to your environment before you start recording. What sounds are likely to get in your way?
- Decide what you want. Do you want to record the general ambience of a scene or is it important to focus on individual voices or sounds?
- Can you control things? If you can turn off or exclude distracting noises, take the time to do it.
- Listen as well as look. Decide to start and stop the camera based on sound as well as sight. Don't stop filming in the middle of a sentence. Wait for noises to die away before you cut.

Sound for editing

If you want to edit your video, you'll need to watch out for sounds that will get in your way.

- Avoid background music – when you cut, the music will cut and it will sound bad. Also, if there's music in the background you can't add your own soundtrack unless you mute the original sound or it will clash.

- Take note of intermittent sounds – traffic noise in the background is OK if it's constant, but an aeroplane passing by every so often will make editing a nightmare as it will keep cutting in and out.

- It often helps to record a minute or so of background noise (a wildtrack) wherever you are. Just turn the camera on while nothing much is happening and leave it for a minute. This will help in the edit as you can use this background noise to cover gaps or edits.

External Microphones

If your camera has an external mic socket – a little plug similar to an earphone socket – try using it. You can get a tie-clip microphone or a simple hand-held mic very cheaply and this will record audio from only a few inches around it. This effectively excludes background noise and will greatly improve your sound.

Zoom microphones are more expensive. These usually mount on your camcorder and record noise only from the direction they're pointed in. These can be great for recording informal conversation as you don't need to hold the mic right in front of the person's nose.

Mini lapel mic

AUTOMATIC AND MANUAL FOCUS, EXPOSURE, AND OTHER SETTINGS

Most cameras come with a choice of automatic and manual functions. There's a simple rule here: if you're getting good footage, leave your camera on its automatic settings. There's no point in overcomplicating your job if you don't need to.

However, when conditions change (or if you expect them to), you'll want to know how to set the manual functions to compensate. Here are a few problems to look out for:

Focus hunting

If there's a lot going on in a shot or if the camera isn't focussing on what you'd like it to focus on, you may need to switch to manual focus.

There will either be a handy button on your camcorder case to do this, or it will be an option in one of the menus.

There are three methods for manually focussing and some cameras offer more than one:

1 **The focus ring** – a ring around the lens of your camera. Just turn the ring to change the focus.
2 **Focus button** – a button which will re-set the auto focus whenever it's pressed. The trick here is to aim your camera directly at something in shot placed at the distance you want to focus on. Press the focus button and then line your shot up.
3 **Touch screen** – if your camera has a touch sensitive viewscreen, you may be able to focus in manual mode simply by touching whatever part of the shot you want to focus on.

Focus ring

HINT: REMEMBER TO RE-FOCUS

If you move the camera significantly, or zoom after focussing in manual mode, then you'll need to re-focus using the same techniques.

Focus manually in dark conditions

Dark conditions

In dark conditions, camcorders start to struggle. This usually means that shots become grainy and the auto focus systems start to fail. If you really can't get any more light on the subject, it's probably best to turn off auto focus and focus manually.

Lighting variations

If you've got very changeable lighting – for example, if you pan from a window to the interior of a room, or if you take the camera from indoors outside while filming, the camera will take time to adjust.

This most commonly causes problems when you're trying to film indoors near a bright window or against a sunlit backdrop – the camera will adjust to the window's light levels and everything inside will be in silhouette.

If this spoils your shot you may need to re-take with the auto-iris (or auto exposure) turned off. Again, this will be a menu item or a button on your camcorder.

Usually when the exposure setting is in manual mode, there will be a control allowing you to lighten or darken the shot. In the case of a bright window you'll have to turn up the exposure, bleaching out the window but giving you a properly exposed foreground.

HINT: BACK-LIGHT COMPENSATION

Some cameras have a back-light compensation control. This, when turned on, will automatically turn up the exposure to avoid silhouetting of your foreground objects.

If you follow the few simple rules you've learnt here, you should be able to return from any shooting project with a collection of strong shots that you'll be able to edit into a compelling video. The more you shoot, the better you'll become at recognising the best shots. Even when you don't have a camcorder to hand, practice thinking through how you'd film any situation you might find yourself in.

3 Shooting situations

How you approach making a video depends very much on what you're pointing the camera at. Here are a few situations in which you might find yourself making a video, along with some quick shooting tips. We'll start with holiday videos and presentations to camera before tackling more complex organised events. By the end of the chapter, you'll even be able to film a wedding or civil union with confidence (and a little help from a friend).

HOLIDAY VIDEOS

You won't want to spend your entire holiday looking through the viewfinder of your camcorder, but you might want to record some memories. It can be different to get the balance right, but the key is to decide what you're going to record and make sure you get enough of a range of shots to create a sequence that stands on its own.

Think of your holiday video as a series of separate videos. Even if your holiday is effectively a single event (like hiking from one place to another) it's still good to treat it as a series of short episodes, each one complete in itself. That way you can avoid just grabbing random shots when something interesting happens, and instead get a range of shots that tell the story of whatever is going on.

As always, sequences of shots rather than single shots in themselves are the key (see page 17).

Sequences of shots tell a story

TIP: FIND THE HUMAN ANGLE

Remember – it's not what's happening that's interesting when you watch the video back, it's the reactions of the people you're with that will define how viewers treat your video. A few shaky shots of dolphins swimming round while people splash about in the water might hold attention for a few seconds, but your child's expression when they come out of the water after swimming with them is priceless.

Don't annoy people by constantly sticking the camera in their face, but know that it's their reactions that will make or break your video. Get those reactions when you can, and if you get a chance, talk to people on-camera.

VIDEOING A PARTY

Parties are usually informal and chaotic. Nobody knows quite what's going to happen when and you need to be ready to react to anything. You won't want to be too intrusive and, of course, you'll want to have a good time yourself. The aim will usually be to put together a few shots after the event's over to give a flavour of the party.

Party shots should be informal

Lights

Party lighting is frequently bad for filming; either because it's too dim or because it's constantly flashing and flickering. You can't do much about this except take note of where the lights in the room are and position yourself so they're on most of the action. If there's a lot of flashing light, it also helps to turn the auto-exposure of your camera off so that it doesn't get confused.

Camera

Focus can also be a problem if everyone's moving quickly, but if you make sure that at least the camera is steady, it will get a chance to focus. Grab your video clips in 20-30 second shots and make sure each is a shot of something or someone in particular, rather than just pointing the camera and hoping something will happen in front of it.

Action

Be constantly aware of what's happening and look out for those moments that make the party interesting. Remember – it's often not what's happening that's important so much as people's reactions to it.

Mini-scenes

Parties, like most events, have a story to them. There are events within them (planned and unplanned) and it's these you need to focus on.

If there's going to be a birthday cake, you'll want to get a shot of it coming in, a shot of the candles being blown out, a shot of it being cut and some shots of it being eaten.

Mini-scenes build a story

If there's a speech, or a game, or a particular dance, you'll want to cover that. Think of these events almost as separate little films in themselves – even if they only last a minute or so – and make sure you get the shots to cover each of them as a story with a beginning, a middle and an end. Do this and you'll be able to break your video up into short, interesting segments instead of it just becoming a montage of shots that don't have anything to do with each other.

TIP: KEEP IT SHORT

There's no need to shoot everything that moves – one shot of people chatting or dancing is pretty much like another. Think about what you want the video to look like, and use your energy to guarantee you get those specific shots rather than trying to capture everything and hope you can make something of it later.

Three shots of a game of pass the parcel tell the story of a birthday party in a far more interesting way than an hour of random footage. The three shots are also far easier to email to your friend in Australia.

A PRESENTATION TO CAMERA

An interview or presentation is a very controllable situation. You can decide where you sit, what the lighting is and exactly what's said. A little preparation can go a long way.

Lights

If the presentation is going to take a while to record, you'll want to be sure the lighting remains the same throughout. Draw the curtains and turn the interior lights on – that way things won't change when the weather alters.

An interview is an easy environment to control

Camera

Turn off auto-focus. The shot is staying the same throughout, so stop the camera from re-focussing distractingly. Turn off auto-exposure as well if you can.

Composition

Take a look at the background. Make it interesting, but uncluttered so that it doesn't distract from the speaker. Above all, make sure the background isn't a lot lighter than the speaker – for example, don't shoot them against a window or the camera will ruin the shot in trying to compensate.

Frame the shot. Set up the shot roughly as a close-up or an MCU (see page 15) – but be prepared to change it if you need to.

Change the shot occasionally. If you want to be able to edit your message, or interview, it helps to occasionally change the shot, zooming in or out. That way the whole thing won't be quite so static, and you'll also be able to cut parts out without causing a jump. However, remember to re-focus the camera each time you change the shot.

Sound

Get good sound. If you've got a plug-in microphone, use it, and use some headphones plugged into the camera to make sure the sound is good before you start. If you don't have an extra microphone, just make sure the camera is close and that the rest of the room is quiet.

Action

Know what you're going to say. If it's you doing the talking, make a few notes. If it's an interview, jot down the questions you're going to ask so you know exactly what's going to happen when you turn on the camera. This will not only make recording easier – your notes will help when you come to edit too.

Rehearse – but not too much. It's good to decide what you're going to say, and it's useful to have notes or even a script. However, don't rehearse too much or you'll end up sounding wooden and dull. Don't be afraid of the odd pause or "umm…". If you completely loose your train of thought you can always re-record.

Talk in whole sentences and if you're interviewing someone, make sure they do too: "Yes" and "no" answers are no good for editing nor are fragments of speech that refer to something you were talking about earlier on (especially if your earlier comments don't appear in the finished video!).

RECORDING AN EVENT

Whether it's a talk, a concert or a sporting event, you're going to have to work around whatever has already been organised. You're also likely to be limited in what you can film and where you can set up. Here's how to get the best from the situation:

Use a tripod

Put your camera on a tripod if you can. You'll get tired of holding it after a few minutes and the shots you take will be much steadier. Also, people tend to respect a tripod and they're far less likely to barge into you or stand in front of you if you look like you're supposed to be there.

Stock up

Make sure you have enough tape, memory and power. If the event is going to go on for a while, make sure you've got access to a plug socket, plenty of batteries and enough tape or camcorder memory to see you through. There's nothing worse than the camera cutting out at a crucial moment.

Use more than one camera

Get two cameras. A two-camera shoot is much, much easier to edit than a one-camera shoot. If you've got two angles on a long event, you can always cut segments out without causing a jump. You can also switch to the alternate camera when the first camera needs to be moved, have its tape changed, or record reaction shots.

If you can, designate one camera to film a "safety shot" – an unmoving wide shot of the whole event from start to finish – while the other camera darts about doing close-ups, reaction shots and everything else. That way you can have as much fun as you like with the roving camera whilst knowing that the stationary camera is always there capturing everything.

A "safety shot" is always a good idea

Don't move too much

Try to move the camera only when you need to. Long, stable shots are much more useful and easier to edit than short wobbly ones. When you need to change shot, decide whether the movement is likely to be used in the finished video. If it is, move slowly and smoothly. If it isn't, move as quickly as you can to minimise the time you need to cut away.

Pay attention to sound

Often, sound will be a problem. The event probably isn't being organised for the benefit of your camera, so bear in mind that the loudest sounds will be those closest to you. That usually means any noises you or the people around you make will be louder on your video than the sounds from the event itself. If you can get close to the action, do so and always use a set of headphones to check what your camera is hearing.

Stay on one side

Get all your shots from one side of the action. The reason for this is simple. Imagine you're recording a football match. If you take a shot from one side of the pitch, your team will be playing from left to right. If you then move to the other side, they'll be playing right to left. Cut the two shots together and the viewer won't know which way the ball is supposed to be moving. This rule doesn't just hold true for sports – imagine watching a conversation in which the speaker appeared to be facing in two different directions!

Get reaction shots

You need to get the main action covered, but make sure you find some time to snatch reaction shots. Pictures of the audience watching, people chatting, or whatever else is going on. Reaction shots are great for covering cuts in the main action, allowing you to shorten a 20-minute speech or add interest to a recording of a live band.

A WEDDING OR CIVIL UNION

Weddings and civil unions are complex and meticulously planned events. In fact they're usually a series of small events one after another throughout a long day, making a wedding video one of the most challenging things you can film with a camcorder.

A wedding videographer's job is different to the photographer's. The photographer is usually there to create a series of memories – snapshots of how a wedding is supposed to look. Consequently, they spend a lot of time setting up the shots they want to get and moving people into position. You're there to record what actually happens, so look for the "real" wedding and don't try to control the action or record the photographer's static shots – just know when things are going to happen and be there when they do.

You really need two cameras with two operators to cover such an event properly (otherwise you'll be rushing around all over the place throughout the day and struggling to create anything when you come to edit). It's equally important to realise that if you're going to make a wedding video then you'll miss out on a lot of the event – so if you have a role in the event yourself, you should delegate the video coverage to someone else. The events and situations that typically occur at a wedding or civil union are listed below, with pointers on how best to capture them. Some of this information will be familiar from the situations above, but the particular challenge of the wedding will provide you with many opportunities to develop your videoing skills.

Preparation

While one camera is being set up at the ceremony to cover the arrivals of the guests, the other should take a few shots of the preparations at the bride or groom's house. As the participants prepare, it's good to get a few informal snatches of conversation or shots of people getting ready to leave.

Make sure you get a shot of the bridal car leaving the house. Meanwhile, shots of the groom waiting at the church or of guests being greeted at the venue can be captured using the other camera.

Arrivals and departures

Time can be a little tight here as the first camera races to get set up inside the venue before the bridal party arrives. The second camera can cover them preparing to enter the venue, then slip in at the back to set up for a wide shot of the whole ceremony.

Preparation shots add interest

The service

While one camera takes a stationary shot of the whole event, the other is free to capture close-ups of the happy couple and other important figures. If you're operating this camera, make sure you know when the important points are going to happen so you can be ready. These can include the vows, the exchange of rings, readings and, if it's a church wedding, sermons. Of course, before you start filming in a place of worship, check that it's allowed.

Make sure you get close-ups of important moments

Vows

Brides and grooms are notoriously bashful when it comes to speaking their vows. If you possibly can, get a microphone close to them, or get a good zoom-mic on your camera.

Leaving

If the reception is taking place at a different location to the service, you'll need to organise your cameras efficiently again so that you can film the happy couple leaving one venue and arriving at the other without having to break the speed limit.

It's particularly important to be there for departures and arrivals; otherwise, when you edit the video it will seem to jump from one event to the next without any real structure. Your audience won't know quite what's going on when or where.

Free time

Between the various events of the wedding or civil union, there will be times when nothing much appears to be happening, where everyone is standing about chatting and waiting to be called in for the next part of the day.

These moments are absolutely pivotal. They're when old friends catch up, when distant family members meet and when people are first introduced. Grab a range of shots of as many different guests as you can because in years to come, it will be these few shots of the "bit players" in the wedding that will rekindle the most poignant memories.

The speeches

Get someone to warn you a minute before the speeches begin – you need to already be recording when the first speaker stands up. Get one camera to cover the speaker while the other roams the audience capturing the reaction of the audience.

Sound can be a problem, so get your main camera as close as possible and give the speaker a microphone if you can.

The reception

Most ceremonies are followed by some kind of party. It's good to grab a few shots from this, and cut it all together over one song. You'll also probably want to cover the couple's first dance.

Recording in the reception will probably be the most challenging part of the day because it's likely to be too dark for your camera. If you can't get hold of an on-camera light, you may have to turn off your camera's auto-focus function and focus manually.

A range of shots will give the flavour of the day

Going home

The couple's leaving the reception is generally an important moment. It's usually less formalised than the entrances and exits during the day, but being there to capture it means there will be a natural ending for your finished video.

Interviews

Throughout the day, take any opportunity to grab people and do short interviews, recording their wishes for the couple and their thoughts on the day. These are great to mix in with the wedding video during the edit.

A shot of the newlyweds leaving the reception gives a natural end to the video

Whatever you're filming, the key is preparation. Everything will go much more smoothly if you know where you're going to stand and what you need to capture before you start. In situations where you don't know what's going to happen next, thinking ahead and being ready is even more vital. There's nothing more frustrating than turning the camera on thirty seconds too late.

4 Getting shots onto your computer

Once you've shot your video, the next step is to transfer it to your computer for editing. Modern camcorders shoot material to tape, disk, hard drive or memory cards (see pages 9–11), and if you expect anyone else to see what you've shot, you'll need to cut it down and either burn it onto DVD or upload it to the Internet.

Keeping your footage in the form it was originally shot isn't really practical since recording formats are constantly changing, and even the most modern is likely to become obsolete in just a few years. The only real solution is to get your memories onto your PC, from where they can be transferred easily onto the latest video format.

How you do this depends on the type of machine your footage was recorded on originally.

TRANSFERRING FOOTAGE FROM A DV OR HDV CAMCORDER

DV and HDV camcorders are specifically designed to work with computers, and capturing footage for editing can be done completely within free programs such as Windows Movie Maker. The program not only allows you to import video directly from the camera tape but also can control the camera's playback. The camera will start and stop, rewind and fast forward under instruction from the computer. All you need to do is put the tape in and tell the program what to record.

Firewire plug

---

1 Plug your DV or HDV camcorder into your computer using the firewire (IEEE1394) socket. Your camera will come with a cable like the one pictured above. The small socket will be found on your camcorder, the larger one on your PC.

 FIREWIRES AND USB PORTS Some camcorders come with a USB port. Don't be tempted to use this instead of a firewire port, it's not a substitute. If your PC doesn't have a firewire socket, you can have one fitted. This is reasonably cheap and they're relatively easy to install, but your computer will need to be opened up, so it's a job for the experts.

---

2 With your computer and camcorder connected, turn on the camera and set it into **playback** mode.

---

3 Load Windows Movie Maker. You can find this in the **All Programs** section of your start menu or in the **Accessories** folder.

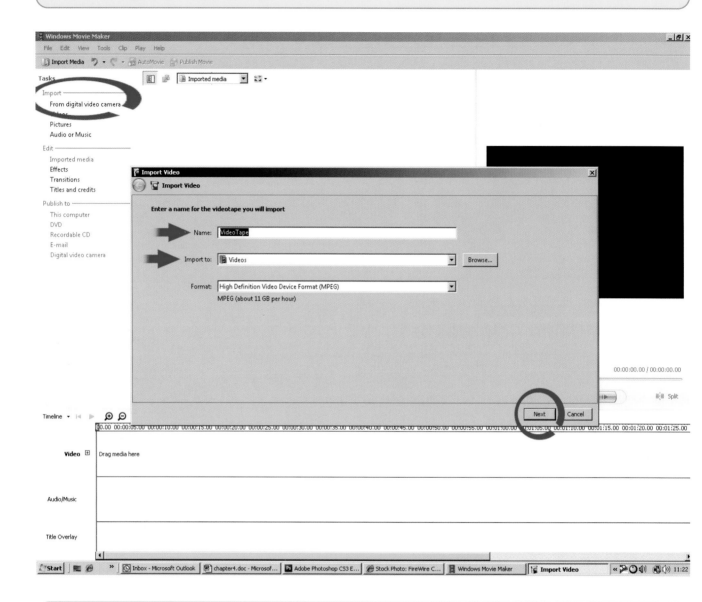

4 Go to the **Import** section of the menu on the left of the screen and select **From digital video camera**. If your camera is correctly connected and turned on, the screen above should appear.

5 You'll be prompted to give your tape a name and a location in which to save the footage. This can be anywhere on your PC, but remember where you put it because once you've finished the project you'll want to delete these huge files.

6 Click **Next** and Windows Movie Maker will automatically rewind your tape to the start and capture it all to disk. The tape will play at normal speed, so how long this takes will depend on how much footage you've recorded.

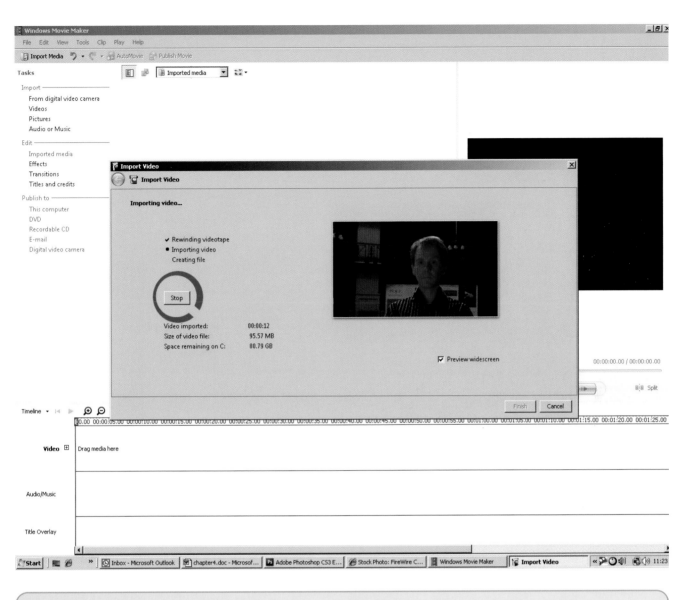

7   You can stop recording at any time by clicking **Stop** or wait for all your footage to be captured. The capture window will then be closed and your footage will be imported into the main window of Windows Movie Maker. From here, you can start editing it.

TRANSFERRING FOOTAGE FROM A DVD CAMCORDER

DVD camcorders record to a DVD disk in a format which can be played back on a TV. This format isn't immediately editable on a PC, so you'll have to transfer your footage before you can use it.

Each camera is different, and not all come with software designed to transfer your video across to your PC. Look for an option for transferring to **avi**, **mov** (**Quicktime**), **mpg** (or **mpeg**) or **wmv** (windows media) formats. If yours doesn't have any of these, you'll need a separate **DVD Ripping** package.

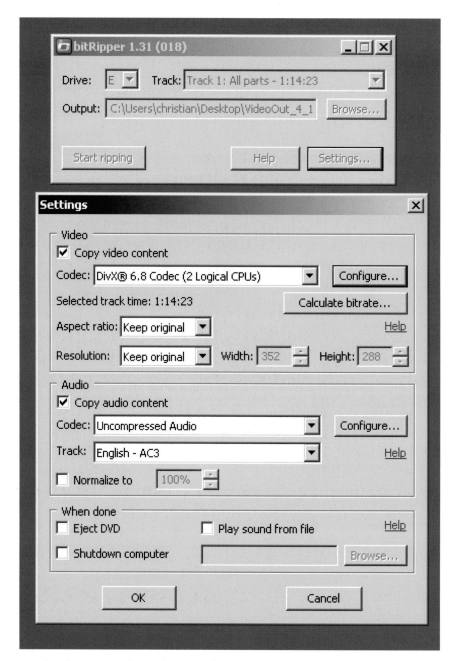

An example of a DVD package that transfers video to an editable file on your hard drive

There are a number of very cheap packages available designed specifically to transfer (or **Rip**) video from DVD to your hard drive. For copyright reasons, most of these packages won't copy commercial DVDs (and you shouldn't attempt to!) but they'll be fine for transferring home-made DVDs or those shot on DVD camcorders.

Once you've transferred your files, you can simply load up Windows Movie Maker and use the **Import video** link at the left-hand side of the window to bring your footage into the package.

TRANSFERRING FOOTAGE FROM A HARD DRIVE CAMCORDER
Some of the newest camcorders on the market are hard drive camcorders. These record to a small hard drive inside the camera. In order to get a lot of footage on the drive, they use a special compression system called **AVCHD**. This format isn't well suited to video editing and many editing packages can't handle it.

Most camcorders come with their own software for transferring **AVCHD** into a format you can edit and you should find it on your camcorder's software CD. If yours doesn't, you may need to buy a package like **VoltaicHD**, which is available online.

Once you've converted your camcorder files to a friendlier format, you can simply open up Windows Movie Maker and import them ready for editing.

TRANSFERRING FOOTAGE FROM A STILLS CAMERA OR MEMORY CARD VIDEO CAMERA

Most modern digital stills cameras now have the ability to record video footage. Quality varies, but footage is recorded onto the same memory card as your still pictures. There are also a few camcorders that record footage straight to a memory card. Video footage takes up a lot more space on a memory card than still pictures, so you need a card of at least 2 gb to store anything more than a few minutes of footage.

RESOLUTION AND FRAME-RATE

Digital still cameras usually allow you to select the quality of images you want to record. The quality is measured by the resolution of the video and its frame-rate. The higher the quality of your video, the more space it will take up and the less you'll be able to fit on a memory card. The higher the resolution, the clearer the picture (see page 12); the higher the frame-rate (not to be confused with the shutter speed), the smoother the movement will be.

Frame rate is measured in frames per second. 12 or 15 frames per second will produce very obviously jerky movement. 24, 25 and 30 frames per second are the normal rates for TV and DVD video.

 GET THE RESOLUTION RIGHT Don't confuse the resolution of still pictures with that of video footage. Your camera will have different settings for each.

HOW TO GET FOOTAGE FROM YOUR STILLS CAMERA ONTO YOUR COMPUTER

1 Place your memory card into a card reader on the PC (see page 37), or plug in your camera (using its **USB** port) and turn it on.

2 If any dialogue boxes appear, they'll be part of the software for your camera. You won't need them, so just close them down.

3 Go to the **Computer** or **My Computer** icon on your start menu and open it up. Locate the new disk drive which will have appeared (it will be called **Removable Disk**) and double click on it. This will open it up.

4 Open any folders you find here until you locate your recorded footage files.

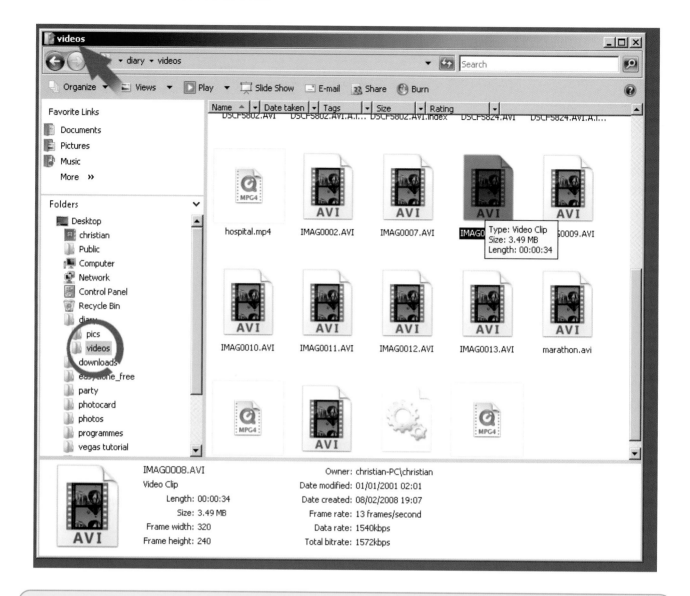

5   Create a new folder on your PC desktop (right click on the desktop and select **New** > **Folder**) and name it **videos**.

6   Drag your footage files from the **Removable Disk** into your new **videos** folder.

7   When you open Windows Movie Maker, you'll be able to locate this new folder and make use of the video files you've copied.

TRANSFERRING FOOTAGE FROM A MOBILE PHONE

Mobile phones usually now come with built-in video recording technology. However, there's no real standard as yet for how to get the video from your phone onto your computer ready for editing.

Each phone has its own software and its own cables. Usually there's a cable which will plug into a computer's USB socket.

Phone USB

Most often, if there isn't dedicated software for downloading your video to a folder on your computer, you can simply plug in the phone. Your phone will appear as an extra **Removable Drive** in the same way that a stills camera does. You can then use the process described above to import and work with your footage.

Phono plugs

TRANSFERRING FOOTAGE FROM AN OLD ANALOGUE CAMCORDER OR VHS

Capturing footage from an old analogue camcorder is a bit trickier. These cameras were never designed to be used with a computer, so you'll need an extra piece of hardware to connect them.

You'll need a device which will convert your old analogue pictures into the digital format accepted by your computer. Such devices are usually called **capture cards** or **video transfer devices**.

These will plug into a USB port on your computer and attach to the phono sockets of your camcorder. Companies making video transfer devices include Pinnacle and Hauppauge. You should expect to pay under £150 ($300) and you'll be able to capture footage not just from any camcorder, but from VHS videotapes too. Many capture devices also allow you to watch and record TV on your computer.

HINT: CONNECTING THE PHONO PLUGS

When connecting up your camcorder make sure you match the right colour plugs. Yellow usually means video, and the red and white plugs are the left and right audio outputs.

Each device will have its own capture software, but the basic procedure is the same:

1 Connect up the camera and the computer.
2 Load up the device's software.
3 Put your camcorder into playback mode.
4 Press **play** on the camcorder and click the software's **record** button.

Your footage will be recorded to disk in a digital format which can be loaded into Windows Movie Maker in the normal way (see page 39).

 REMEMBER WHERE YOU'VE STORED YOUR FOOTAGE Make sure you know which folder your capture device is using to store your video clips – you'll need to find them again when you load up Windows Movie Maker.

HOW TO TELL IF YOUR CAMCORDER IS ANALOGUE

Analogue camcorders use **8mm**, **hi8**, **SVHS**, **VHSC** or **VHS** tapes. They don't use **DV** tapes. Any camcorder purchased before 2000 will probably be analogue. Analogue camcorders usually produce inferior picture quality and don't have modern USB or Firewire plug sockets. If your camcorder has a firewire (IEEE1394) socket, then it's a digital machine.

TRANSFERRING FOOTAGE FROM A WEBCAM

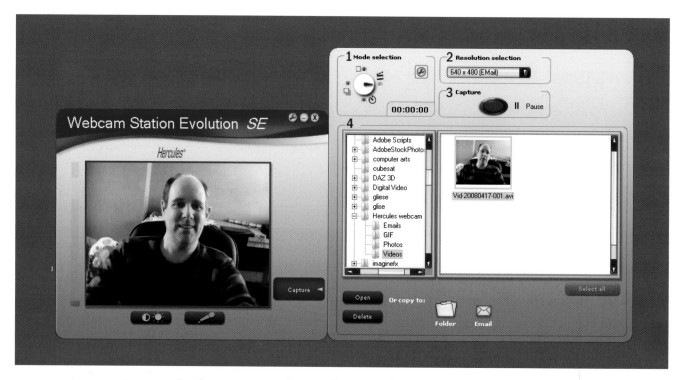

An example of a top range webcam software package used for recording videos

Webcams are already connected to and controlled through your computer. Your video editing package won't be able to control your webcam, but if the device has been installed correctly, there will be software on your PC already to record from it.

Make sure you've got a microphone connected as well if you want to record audio and take a note of where on your PC your webcam videos are being recorded to, so that you can import them to your editing package later on.

However you get it there, having your memories on your hard drive means they're instantly accessible. You don't need to root around in cupboards to find them and, while technology changes, they'll never become obsolete. This in turn means you'll eventually build up quite a collection of video and it's worth making sure you name everything as you capture it and organise it into folders you'll recognise in years to come. It's also well worth considering buying an external hard drive just for video footage; that way it won't clog up your PC and you'll be able to move it easily whenever you replace your computer.

5 Your first edit

In this chapter, you'll discover how to take video and still images stored on your computer and turn them into edited movies. You'll learn to cut out unwanted sections, combine clips into longer sequences and make slideshows from still photos.

TIP: DON'T PANIC

Whatever you do in cutting, editing, re-arranging, adding and deleting video clips or still photos within Windows Movie Maker cannot harm your original footage or photos. Nothing done in Windows Movie Maker is **EVER** saved to your original media files. You can safely shorten a video clip, rotate a photo or do anything else without causing any harm to the files on your disk.

All the changes you make are stored in the Windows Movie Maker project file and nowhere else – and when you publish your finished project, a new movie file is created on disk containing the edit you've created. Even then, the material in it is just copies – your original files remain just as they were.

So feel free to play around and try things out.

EDITING A PHOTO SLIDESHOW

Our first look at video editing won't contain any video at all. Here, you'll be working entirely with still photos and using them to create a video slideshow.

 WHAT YOU NEED AND HOW TO GET IT To complete this tutorial, you'll need a selection of photos on your hard drive and you'll need to know which folder they're in. The photos can be any size and any shape, but pictures that fit roughly into the shape of a TV screen will work best.

Transferring stills from a digital camera or CD

1 If your photos are on a digital camera, then you can connect the camera to your computer using the **USB** socket and turn it on, or remove the camera's memory card and place it into a card reader.

HINT: CARD READERS

There are card readers on most modern printers and many PCs have them built in. Usually you'll see a collection of two or three rectangular slots because there are several different types of card. Just choose the one that fits your card and push it in firmly.

---

2 Often, just inserting the card will prompt your computer to bring up a window (depending on the software you have installed). Simply close these windows and instead select the **Computer** or **My Computer** icon from your Start menu. Your camera or card will have appeared as a **Removable Disk** with a new letter (probably **E:**). Open this, and keep opening the folders which appear inside it until you find your photos.

3 Now, create a new folder on your PC desktop (right click on the desktop and select **New > Folder**) and name it **photos**.

4 Back in the folder that currently contains your photos, select all your images (by clicking on one of them and then pressing `Alt` + `A`) and drag them onto your new file. Your computer will now make a copy of all your photos and save them in the folder on your desktop; you can remove or delete the photos on your camera.

TIP: USING PHOTOS FROM A FILM CAMERA

If you want to make a slideshow using photos taken with a film camera, get them developed commercially and ask for the digital images to be put onto a CD (you can also do this with images from a digital camera). You can then simply put the CD into your CD drive, open it up from your **Computer** or **My Computer** window (right click on the CD icon and select **explore**) and copy the files across as above.

YOUR FIRST LOOK AT WINDOWS MOVIE MAKER

Open up Windows Movie Maker. You can find this in the **All Programs** section of your **Start** menu or in the **Accessories** folder.

Windows Movie Maker is a video editing package. It allows you to take all kinds of media (video clips, still images, graphics and sound files) and trim them down or re-order them to create video productions.

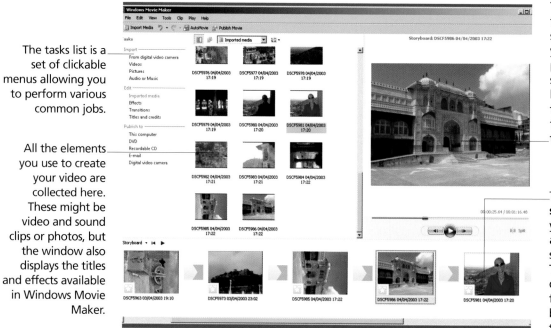

The tasks list is a set of clickable menus allowing you to perform various common jobs.

All the elements you use to create your video are collected here. These might be video and sound clips or photos, but the window also displays the titles and effects available in Windows Movie Maker.

The **monitor** – this is just like a TV screen and displays your edited programme. The slider at the bottom allows you to move back and forward through the programme.

The **timeline** or **storyboard**. Here, your programme is assembled as a sequence of shots. There are two different "looks" for this window, but they both have the same function.

Windows Movie Maker automatically opens with any clips you've previously imported ready to work with. We want to start from scratch, so if there are any items in the middle window, simply select and delete them (this won't erase them from your hard drive).

IMPORTING INTO WINDOWS MOVIE MAKER

1 Go to the **Tasks** panel at the left of the screen and select **Pictures** from the **Import** menu. A dialogue box will appear. Navigate to the **Photos** folder you've created on your desktop.

2 Now select all the pictures (click on one, and choose Alt + A) and then click import. The pictures will now be brought in and thumbnails will appear in the middle of your screen. If you've imported a lot of pictures, you'll be able to scroll through them with the vertical bar to the right of your images.

PLACING PICTURES ON THE STORYBOARD

1 It's now time to make your first edit. Select the picture you'd like to appear first in your slideshow and drag it into the first slot in the storyboard window at the bottom left of the screen.

TIP: VIEWING YOUR PICTURES

In Windows Movie Maker, you can click once on any picture along your storyboard to see a larger version of it in the monitor window.

 MAKE SURE YOU'RE IN THE RIGHT MODE If the bottom of your screen doesn't look like the image above, it's probably in Timeline mode – We'll meet the **Timeline** a bit later on, but for now you can switch back to storyboard mode with the button at the top left of the timeline window.

2 Select another shot and drag it into the next box of the storyboard in just the same way. This creates a second edit.

3 Now go to the controls underneath the monitor window. Drag the blue **playback** head marker all the way over to the left. This rewinds your show to the beginning. Now hit the **play** button underneath it. You'll now see your first picture for 5 seconds, followed by a cut to your second shot.

4 Now's a good time to save your edit. Choose **Save Project** from the **File** menu, name your project "slideshow" and click **OK**. It's important to save your project regularly.

5 Carry on dragging pictures from the middle window down onto the storyboard. When you've filled up all the slots, simply drag the slider at the bottom to display more. You can put in as many pictures as you like.

TIP: RE-ORDERING YOUR PICTURES

If you decide you don't want a picture in the slideshow, just click on it on the storyboard and hit the
 button on your keyboard. If you want to change the order in which pictures appear, simply drag pictures forward or backwards along the storyboard. It's as easy as that.

6 Play back your slideshow often to check how it's looking.

! **SELECT THE STORYBOARD** If you hit play and you don't get what you expect, it's probably because you haven't selected the storyboard. **Playback** will start from whichever shot is selected when you click play. So if you've got the last photo selected, there won't be anything to play.
You can either drag the blue playback head backwards through the production, or simply click on the first shot in the storyboard to start playback from the beginning.

Adding transitions

Once you've put in all the pictures you want, it's time to give the slideshow a bit more style.

1 Go to the **Edit** menu at the left hand side of the screen and select **Transitions**. Your library of pictures will be replaced with a set of icons showing different ways to get from one shot to the next. Try clicking on one and then hitting the **play** button. You'll get a demonstration of how the transition looks.

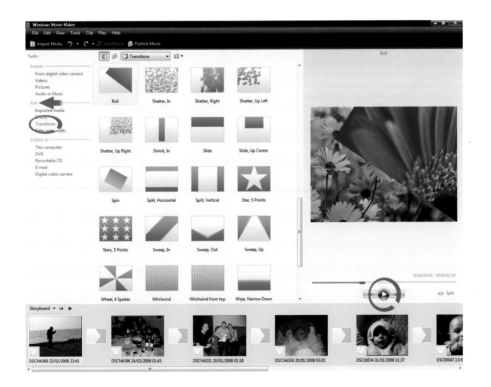

2 To use a transition in your slideshow, simply drag it to the small icon in between two pictures on your storyboard, then hit **play** to see what you've done.

3 If you don't like the effect, you can replace it with another transition or simply select it and hit the ⌦ key.

TIP: KEEP IT SIMPLE

Try to limit your use of transitions. If you make every shot change using a different transition, the effect can be distracting and unpleasant. Stick to one or two throughout your show. If you watch TV, you'll notice professionals rarely use anything other than the simple Fade transition.

---

4 Once you've added all the transitions you want, switch back to viewing your pictures. Go to the **Edit** menu at the left of the screen and select **imported media**. You can now carry on adding and replacing pictures.

Rotating a picture

Here we've put in a picture that was shot with the camera on its side. We'll need to rotate it to make it look right.

1 Go to the **Edit** menu again, but this time select **Effects**. The pictures will be replaced with a series of special effects which can be applied to anything on your storyboard.

2 Select the **Rotate 90** or **Rotate 270** effect (depending whether you need a clockwise or anticlockwise rotation) and drag it onto the shot.

3 The picture should now be shown the right way up.

TIP: UPSIDE DOWN PICTURES

If the picture appears upside down, just select the **effects** icon (the little star that appears at the bottom left of your picture icon in the storyboard – circled in red) and hit `Del`. You can then drag in a replacement effect to rotate it in the right direction.

Creating movement

There are other even more interesting effects available in Windows Movie Maker. Choose the **Ease In** effect and drag it to a photo on your storyboard.

Now play it back. The effect has created a slow zoom into the photo. This helps to give your photos movement and adds interest.

TIP: PLAY AROUND WITH EFFECTS

As well as the **Ease In** effect, try the **Ease Out** and **Pan and Zoom** effects to create a range of different movements. Select whichever will work best for each photo in your slideshow.

Publish your movie

Once you've finished your edit and you're happy with the way it looks, you'll want to create a version you can play back without Windows Movie Maker or to give to other people.

1   Go to the **Publish To** menu at the left hand side of the screen and select **This Computer**. Name your movie and select browse to locate a folder in which to put your finished movie (we've chosen the desktop so that it's easy to find).

2   Click **Next** and you'll be offered a choice of quality options – accept the one that's suggested and click **Publish**. Your slideshow will now be created (this can take a while depending on the length of the movie).

3   When it's finished publishing, you can close Windows Movie Maker and locate your file on your hard drive (if you've placed it on the desktop, this should be straightforward). Double click on the icon and it will play back.

HINT: PUBLISHING TO A DVD

If you want to know how to put your slideshow onto a DVD, take a look at the tutorial on page 75.

YOUR FIRST VIDEO EDIT

Editing a video is almost exactly the same as creating a slideshow. You're working with moving images rather than still ones so there are a few differences, but the process is the same. Remember to select and delete the images shown when you load up Windows Movie Maker – they'll be left over from your last edit and you won't need them here.

Importing videos

Again, we have to import some files to work with. Go to the **Videos** section of the **Import** menu at the left of the screen. A browser window will appear; use this to find your video footage. If you've captured it as we did on page 29, it will be in your **Videos** folder within the **My Documents** folder.

Creating clips

If you've shot your footage with a hard drive camcorder or a stills camera recording to a memory card, you'll have each shot as a separate video file.

If your video came from a tape camcorder, or from some other source, it will import as one long clip containing all the shots together.

This makes it a little tricky to find the shot you're looking for when editing, so we'll need to create some clips. No problem: simply right click on the shot once you've imported it and select **Create Clips**. Windows Movie Maker will scan through your file attempting to work out where shots start and end. It will then display each shot as a separate icon instead of a single long file.

HINT: CREATING CLIPS

Scanning can take a long time – Windows Movie Maker has to check every frame to see how different it is from the next one. On this basis it decides whether there has been a cut.

This means the package can get confused. For example, if you shoot at a film premiere where there are camera flashes going off all the time, you might find one shot gets cut into several pieces.

Don't worry too much about this – you can easily convert them into a single clip by selecting all the parts, and then choosing **Combine** from the **Clip** menu.

Drag in a clip

1   Choose the first shot you want to use and drag it down to the storyboard just as you did with the still images (see page 39). It will appear in the storyboard and where it can be played back.
2   Drag in the clip you want to follow the first shot and just as in the slideshow tutorial, this will appear next to it. Again, just as in the previous section, you can add, remove and re-arrange your footage.

Playing back your footage, you should see the shots you've placed on the storyboard edited together. However, right now you have the entirety of each clip in your storyboard. It's more than likely that you'll want to trim the clips, taking off unwanted footage from the beginning and end of each shot.

Using the timeline mode

Click on the word storyboard at the top left of the storyboard window and switch the display to timeline mode.

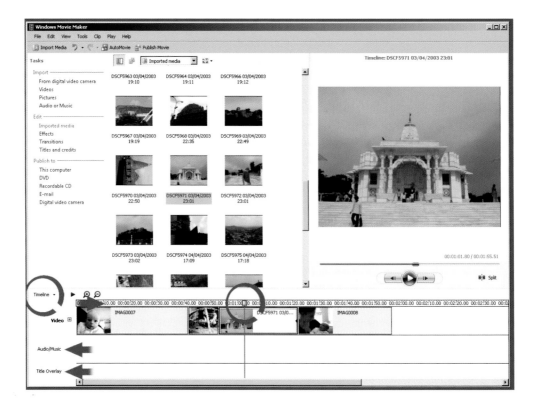

The timeline is just another way of looking at the clips in your storyboard. Your clips are now shown as rectangles arranged on a video track. Above this, a time counter is displayed so you can see exactly how long each clip lasts.

Below the clip track, there are two more tracks – where you can add extra sound and titles. We'll take a look at these later.

The green vertical line through the timeline is the playback head. By dragging on the top of it, you can move it back and forward through the production. This is useful for finding exactly the right moment to place an edit. The monitor displays the frame on which the playback head rests.

Trimming your clips

1 **Timeline** mode offers you a little more control than the **Storyboard** display. Here, you can lengthen or shorten your clips. Just select the clip and drag on the left or right-hand edges of it on the timeline.

2 If you started filming a little before the action occurred, you can just drag the left-hand edge of the clip to the right to trim the beginning. If on the other hand, you want to end the shot a little earlier, just drag the right-hand side to the left.

3 Play back the shot and you can see what you've done. If you don't like the position of the cut, you can always lengthen the clip again by dragging the ends of the clip back out to where they were. The key thing to remember is nothing is ever lost – you can always re-edit to bring the footage you remove back.

STARTING AND FINISHING YOUR CLIP

There is another way to set the start and end points of your clip. Drag the **playback head** to the point at which you want the shot to start. Select **Trim Beginning** from the **Clip** menu, then drag the head to the frame on which you want to end the shot. Select **Trim End**. This method is most useful when you want to be very specific about the start and end points. You can even move the **playback head** back and forth one frame at a time with the frame buttons below the monitor screen.

HINT: ADDING CLIPS IN TIMELINE MODE

You can add shots in timeline view just as easily as you can in storyboard view; simply drag them onto the timeline. You can also swap them around and delete them in just the same way.

TIP: USING THE ZOOM BUTTONS

If your timeline gets too long, or if you need to do extremely fine editing, you can zoom in or out with the zoom buttons at the top of the timeline. These allow you to see more of your edit or focus in on just a few seconds, but they don't alter your production in any way.

PLAYBACK SPEED You might notice playback of your footage slowing down as you add transitions and effects, especially if you're working with **High Definition** footage. Adding effects means your computer is having to work extra hard to process and play back the video. This leads to stuttering and slow playback.

When your movie is finished, it won't look like this. Playback of your edited film will be smooth and regular, so don't worry too much about how things look in the monitor window.

Add a transition

Just as with still images, we can add transitions to video clips.

> **1** Go to the **edit** menu on the left-hand side of the screen and select **Transitions**. Drag your chosen transition effect between any two clips.
>
> **2** It's easy to make a transition longer or shorter, too. Just select the second clip and slide it backwards into the first. The bigger the overlap you create, the longer the transition will last. You can see the length of the overlap on the timeline.

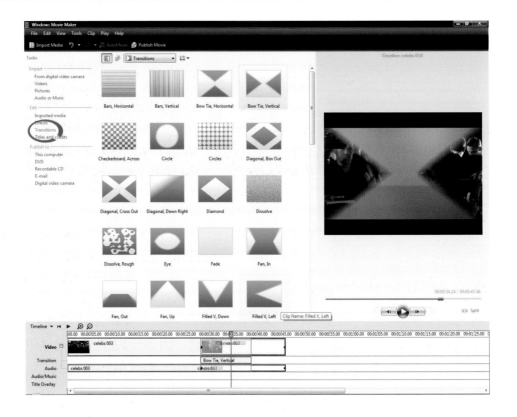

Finish off

A good way to start and end your movie is to fade in and out from a black background. To do this, simply select the first clip on your timeline, right click on it and choose **Fade In**. Now pick the last shot and choose **Fade Out**.

Make your movie

Finally, once you're happy with your edit, choose **This Computer** from the **Publish To** menu, give your video a name and save it in a location where you can easily find it.

By now you'll have all the tools you need to create a basic video edit. You should be able to use still and moving images to construct a scene on the timeline and to render out that scene as a finished video production. However, there's a lot more to video editing than simply assembling shots – and in the next few chapters, we'll learn some of the more advanced techniques.

6 Telling stories with video

In the last chapter we came to grips with the basics of how to assemble an edit – how to physically arrange one shot after another to create a video sequence. This is a bit like learning to write: being able to shape the letters and spell words is important, but it's just as important to understand how to put words together to communicate. Just as words have language and grammar and structures which allow you to tell stories, video also has structures of its own.

STORYTELLING

TIP: USE YOUR VIDEO TO TELL A STORY

Video making is about storytelling. The single most important thing to remember when making a video is that whenever you pick up your camcorder, what you're aiming to do is to tell a story.

What people watching your video are interested in is how each new shot and each new scene that you introduce tells them more about what's going on or progresses your story.

If home movies are dull, it's almost always because they haven't been edited with any kind of story. There's nothing wrong with beautiful shots of mountains, for example, but if you don't know why you're being shown the mountain, what the shot is leading to or what it's telling you that you don't already know, then you'll get bored quickly. As a viewer, if you're given a context by the way the programme is edited so that you know why you're looking at the mountain – whether it's important or just part of the scenery, what you're supposed to be feeling about it and whether it's half way through the production or a minute from the end – then you'll start to trust the video maker and become interested in watching.

TIP: THINK ABOUT THE SHOT SEQUENCE

Before you start editing, take some time to watch your footage and think about what you're trying to say with the video, what the important parts are, and how you plan to arrange them.

Most of the time, this will be fairly obvious. Most of the time, the order in which you've recorded shots will be a good guide to the order in which they need to appear. However, don't just dump everything you've shot onto the timeline. Be very strict with yourself about which shots fit together to tell your story and don't be afraid to get rid of some of your favourite shots if you decide they don't fit with the story you're telling.

MAKING A SCENE

Think of a scene as a mini-story within your video. If you're editing a holiday video, one scene might be the journey to your destination. Another might be an excursion. Think of each scene individually; (often professional editors will edit scenes separately, bringing into their editing package only the footage they need for the scene they're working on and then producing a finished video clip of each one).

Decide what's going to happen in each scene and give it a beginning, a middle and an end. For example: a scene of a journey might start with packing suitcases, continue with scenery from the journey and end with arrival at your destination. The sequence needn't be complicated – it just has to tell the audience something new with each additional shot.

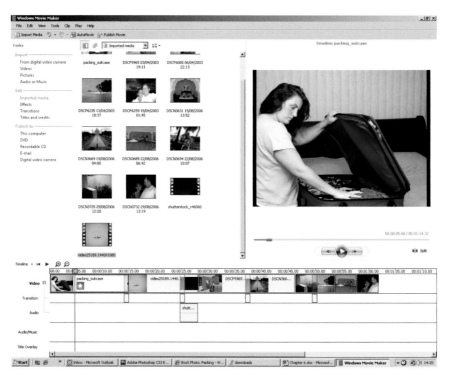

To create a story, shoot a scene that shows the beginning of the journey

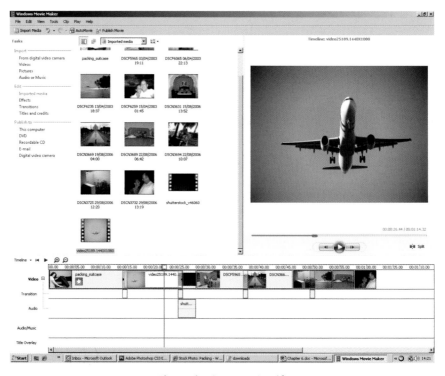

Show the journey itself

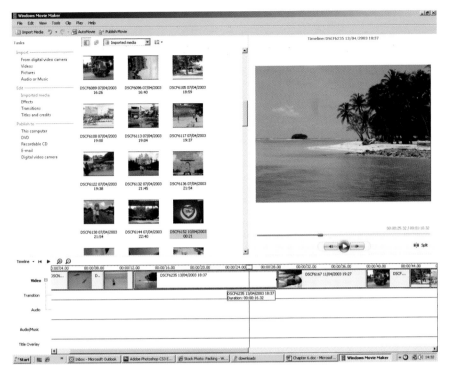

Arriving at the destination

Once you start thinking about your video in terms of scenes, things become a lot easier. You can work out how long you think each scene should last and make sure that one isn't disproportionately longer than the rest just because you had more opportunity to film. You can decide how each scene fits in with the overall video to tell the story. You can work out how long your finished production will be so that you don't end up turning a day at the seaside into a 4-hour epic.

In addition, you can decide whether there's room for particular shots or whether you have to throw them out.

TIPS: HOW TO CONSTRUCT A SCENE

BME – Beginning, Middle and End. Scenes, just like stories, generally start by introducing a situation, asking a question or creating a mystery. The middle of the scene explores what happens next, and the end of the scene answers the question, resolves the mystery or ends the situation.

Drama – try to edit to increase dramatic tension. If you've got a shot of a church filling with people, and a shot of a bride getting ready, you can easily cut back and forth to make it look as though the groom is waiting nervously while the bride is still having her hair done – despite the fact that in reality she arrived just a few minutes after him. Always be on the lookout for opportunities of making the viewer feel as though there's a chance things could all suddenly go very differently.

TIPS: HOW TO CONSTRUCT A SCENE

Close-ups and long shots – use a combination of wide shots to give an overview of what's going on in a scene and where everyone is, and close-ups to show the detail of what's happening.

Start long – starting with a wide establishing shot, then cutting to close ups is often a good way of assembling a scene.

Use cut-aways – cut-aways are shots of something not central to your scene which can be slipped in if you need to edit time or create a pause. For example, if you want to remove a dull section of a sporting event, simply cut to the reactions of the crowd and then cut back. The viewer won't feel they've missed anything.

Use cut-ins – cut-ins are close-ups that illustrate the action. If you've got a video of someone cooking, a cut-in of the saucepan being stirred or ingredients being chopped can give a useful explanation of what's going on.

Cut on movement – cuts can often look a lot more natural if you cut during a movement. For example, if a cricketer takes a swing at a ball in a wide shot, you can cut to a close-up of the moment the ball is struck, then to a third shot of the ball flying through the air to be caught. The fact that all three shots came from different parts of the game won't be noticed if you get the edit right.

Cuts and mixes – try to use mostly straight cuts rather than fancy transitions. Mixes can sometimes be useful at the beginning or end of a scene, or when you want to convey the passing of time or make a transition gentler.

A long shot allows viewers to orientate themselves

Once you've established your shot, you can go in closer to pick out interesting details

Use cut-ins to show the important action of a scene

EDITING SPEECH

If you're editing speech – whether it's a presentation to camera, an interview or even a dramatic film scene, there are a few simple rules to follow:

Cut to the speech

The audio is the most important thing to get right so start by editing so that the speech makes sense. Use the **split** tool (at the right-hand side of the timeline) to split long speeches into individual phrases so you can remove the unwanted sections more easily. You can go in later on to clean up the visual side, placing extra shots and adjusting the edit to make the visuals work.

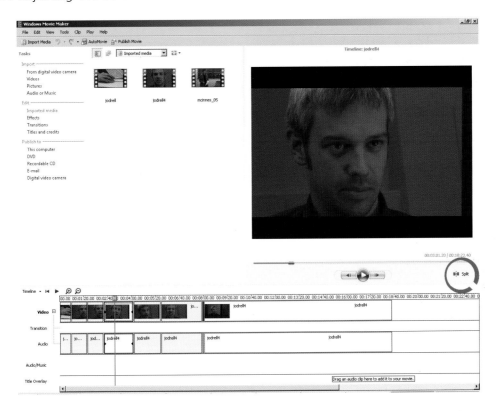

Paper edit

If you're editing an interview, you might have an hour of footage and only want the odd little bit. Such long takes can be very cumbersome to work with in an editing package, so it helps to watch the footage first, and note down the time when interesting or important things are said. That way you can easily find and cut out the sections you want.

Jump cuts

The chances are you'll have recorded any speech in its entirety and will want to cut it down. If you've only got one shot, when you cut out a portion you'll get a jump in the video even though it won't be noticeable on the audio track. These jumps need to be covered and there are a couple of ways of doing this:

Cut-ins and cut-aways – dropping an extra shot without sound over the cut is the best way to cover it. To do this in Windows Movie Maker you'll need to drag short shots in between your clips. If you've planned the shooting well, you'll have taken a range of shots which can be used in this way. Close-ups of hand gestures, reaction shots of an audience, shots of the room in which the filming is taking place, or even stock footage or still images of whatever the speaker is talking about all make good covering shots.

Fast fades – if no cut-away material exists, or if you need an instant transition, you can create a very fast (half a second or less) fade between the two shots. Simply drag in the fade from your transitions list and click the **+** button next to the Video track at the left of the timeline. This reveals the transitions track and allows you to drag on the transition to shorten it.

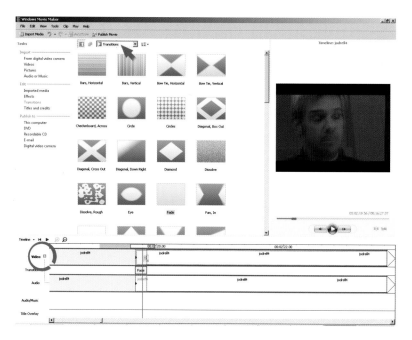

Pauses – if there's a definite end to what the speaker is saying and they're about to start on another subject, it's often a good idea to cut for a few seconds to something else. This brief interlude gives the viewer a moment to reflect on what's been said and get ready for a change of subject.

EDITING ACTION

Action can be anything from a battle scene in a Hollywood epic to somebody making a cup of tea or coffee. If the main focus of the scene is somebody doing something rather than saying something, then it's an action scene. Action scenes have their own problems and challenges, the following guidelines will help you to make the most of your footage.

Follow the action

There may be many things going on at once in a scene. Choose what you think is most interesting and important and follow that. This may be dictated to you by the shots you have to work with, but it's worth keeping in mind while you edit. Remember, every time you place a clip on your timeline, ask yourself how the shot is advancing the story you're trying to tell.

Think how each shot helps to tell the story

Look for gaps

Unless you've shot the scene very comprehensively with a number of cameras or re-shot a number of times, at points you will miss moments of action. You might have filmed a tennis match, for example, but were positioned behind one player, so didn't get to film the winning shot on the other side of the net. You'll need to think of ways to cut around the missing moments (in this case, shots of expectant spectators overlaid with the sound of a tennis ball hitting racquet strings might work). The important thing is to know where the gaps are and think carefully about how to fill them rather than simply arranging the footage you've got together in chronological order.

Cut aways fill gaps in the action

Movement

As explained on page 52, cutting in the middle of a movement can create a smooth transition and add to the action in a video. However, this only works if you've got (or can create) more than one angle on the same movement. If you can't, you'll be faced with either having much longer shots than you might like, or making greater use of cut-aways.

Timing and pace

Generally in an action sequence, the shorter the shots are, the more exciting the pace of the action. However, that's not a hard and fast rule and learning to use and vary pace in your editing is an important skill. High action scenes like a fight, or a dance music video often contain shots that are cut down to less than a second each. However, a video in which every shot is just a few frames long would be unwatchable.

It's all about proportion and rhythm. A longer shot gives the audience a chance to see what's actually going on, or work out how everything fits together. It also allows important time to see who's thinking what.

For example, if you're editing children building sandcastles, then lots of rapid close-ups of sand being shovelled and piled give a great feeling of things being done. However, cut for a few seconds to a wider shot of the scene – or even a close up of one of the children deciding where to plant the next castle – and suddenly the scene has perspective, and a story.

Music

If you have a scene where the audio isn't that important, overlaying some music is often a good idea. The choice of music can be crucial in determining the atmosphere of the scene, so choose carefully. If you are using music, it's often a good idea to lay that onto the timeline first, and then arrange your action around it. That way you can try to make cuts occur on the music's beats and use the music to set a rhythm for the cuts in your edit.

The techniques we've learnt here aren't just technical ones – they're the creative concepts editors use to build tension and add interest to their productions. Practice them and you'll soon find your video edits becoming sharper and more watchable. As you begin to recognise the elements of a good scene within your raw footage, your editing will become faster and more efficient.

7 Advanced techniques

When editing, there's a lot more you can do with your video projects beyond cutting and trimming shots and arranging them in order. In this chapter we'll be looking at a few of the more advanced editing tools available in Windows Movie Maker, including the ability to add animated titles and captions and apply special effects filters.

ADDING TITLES

Adding titles, text screens and captions to your videos is a great way of clarifying what's going on, adding extra information or providing credits. Windows Movie Maker allows you to create still or moving text which can be placed on the Timeline in just the same way as still images or video clips.

Basic Titles

Let's start by putting a simple title screen at the start of our production. (You can create a new film here, or use one of the productions you created in the last chapter).

> **1** Go to the **Edit** menu at the left of the screen and select **Titles and credits**. You'll be offered a list of different types of titles; choose **Title at the beginning**. This will bring up a text box at the top left of the screen into which you can type your title. The text box is divided into two sections. The top is for the main title. The bottom section allows you to add a subtitle if you want to.

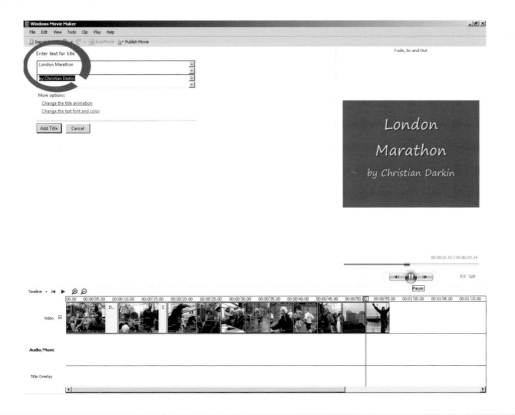

2 You don't have to add a subtitle, but you can add a second line of text, an episode number or even your own credit if you wish. As soon as you hit return, or click outside of the box, your title is displayed as an animation in the monitor window at the right of the screen. The main title fades in first, then after a couple of seconds, the subtitle appears. Both titles then fade out together. If you want to see the title again, you can click the **play** button underneath the monitor.

3 And that's it. If you click **Add title**, your caption will be added as a media clip at the start of your show on the Timeline.

4 You can lengthen or shorten the title just as you would with a still or movie clip by dragging on its end points on the Timeline. You can delete it by selecting it and hitting ⌦ and you can re-edit its text by double clicking on it.

Animation and Colour

There are a lot more options for titling beyond the basic tutorial we've just completed. Underneath the text boxes, there are two links: **Change the title animation** and **change the text font and colour**.

1 **Change the title animation** offers you dozens of different options for animating your text. You can do everything from flying in your title as the headline in a newspaper to fading, scrolling, spinning or zooming it into and out of shot.

Feel free to experiment with a few of the animations – until you hit **Add title**, nothing in your Timeline will be changed. The animations are preset, so you can't change anything about them – all you have to do is pick one, and Movie Maker will do the rest.

2   The second option, **Select title font and colour**, allows you to customize the look of the text itself. Select it and you will be presented with a set of controls similar to those in a word processor.

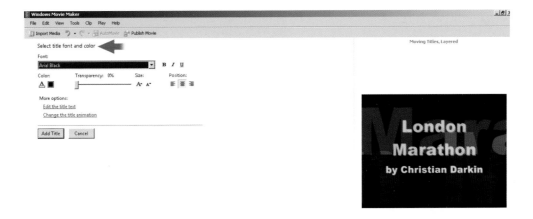

- The top row allows you to pick a font from a dropdown list – click on the control and you'll get a list of all the type styles on your computer.
- This isn't very useful unless you know what they look like, so press the up and down arrows on your keyboard, to scroll through the available typefaces. Windows Movie Maker will then show them in action in your monitor window.
- The second row of controls are for setting the colour, size and alignment of your text. Select the first button to choose the colour of the text. The second will let you pick the background colour. There's also a transparency slider for fading the text in and out, followed by two buttons for making the text bigger or smaller.
- Finally, the last three buttons allow you to choose whether you want the text centred, aligned to the left or aligned to the right.

Title overlays

You can also superimpose your title over an existing piece of video footage. You might want to do this if you want to put a person's name underneath their picture, add extra information to a photograph or video clip or place a video's title over its first shot.

1 Go to the Timeline and select the clip over which you want to superimpose your caption. From the Edit menu at the left of the screen, choose **Titles and credits** as you did with the basic title.
2 This time, select the **Title on the selected clip** option.
3 The text window we've met before will appear again, allowing you to type in your caption, with a subtitle if you want one.

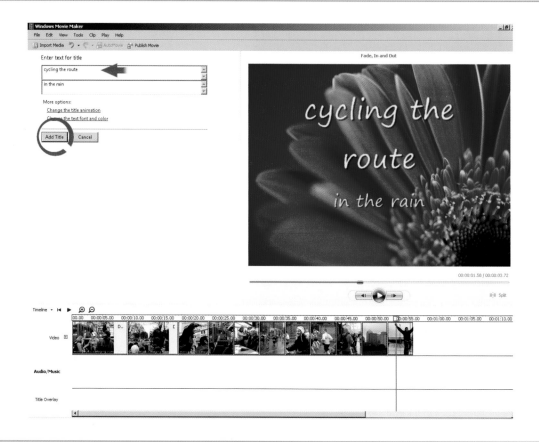

4 As before, the **animation** and **font colour** options are available. This time, however, the **background colour** option in the **font options** is disabled (there is no background here – the text is overlaid onto your video clip).
5 On the monitor, your title is shown superimposed onto a substitute picture (in our example, it's a flower). This gives you an idea of how your caption will look.
6 When you've perfected the title and animation, simply click **Add title** and your caption will be superimposed over the clip of your choice.
7 Look at the **Timeline**. This time, instead of being placed in the **video** track, you'll find your title in the **Overlay** track.

Anything placed in the overlay track will be superimposed on top of whatever is in the video track. The title is shown as a rectangle on the **Timeline** which can be lengthened, shortened, moved or deleted in the normal way.

ROLLING CREDITS

Creating a set of credits at the end of your movie is just as easy as adding a title.

1 Again, go to **Titles and credits** – this time, select the **Credits at the end** option.

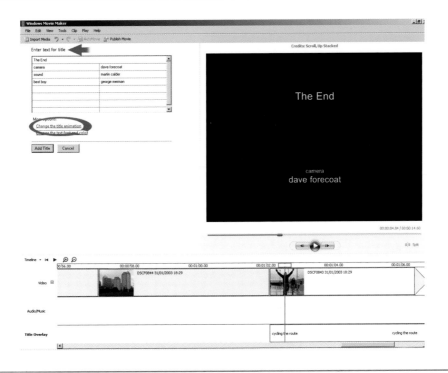

2 This time, there's a whole table of text fields for you to fill in. They're in two columns: the left hand column creates small text and right hand one produces larger text.

3 You can add as many lines as you like and adjust the font and colours as before. By default, your text will scroll up the screen, but if you select **Change the title animation** you can add a number of more unusual credit animations.

TIP: ANIMATING YOUR TITLE

When you change the length of a title on the Timeline, the animation on that title is sped up or slowed down automatically.

TOP TITLING TIPS

1 Colour: professional titles are rarely anything other than black or white. Bright colours rarely look good and carry the danger of clashing with anything else on screen.

2 Contrast: take a look at the background on which you want to place your titles. If it's dark, use a light colour and vice-versa. If your titles don't stand out, an audience won't bother trying to read them.

3 Size: use big, bold titles and don't try to get too much on the screen. Limit yourself to a single sentence at the most. Even subtitled movies have only a couple of lines of large text at a time.

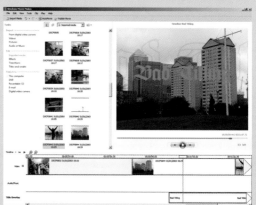

4 Clarity: there are a lot of fussy, complicated fonts out there and most aren't suitable for moving words. Use something simple: **Times New Roman** or **Arial** are good choices. They're classic, easily readable and they won't look dated or tacky.

VOICEOVERS AND MUSIC

One great way to spice up your video is to add music and narration to it. Windows Movie Maker allows you to do both.

Music

You can bring a slideshow to life by adding a little music. Background music can also create a great atmosphere for a video, or provide audio for an opening theme or closing credits.

Music clips are added just like video clips and can be manipulated in just the same way. They can be moved backwards and forwards along the Timeline and shortened and lengthened in just the same way as video footage.

Music on your computer

If your music is already on your computer, adding it to your video is really simple.

1 Go to **Import** in the left hand menu and select **Audio or Music**.

2 The browser window will open and allow you to locate your music on your hard drive just as you'd locate pictures or video clips. Once you've selected your music, click **OK** and it will appear in your **imported media** window alongside your video clips.

3 Now drag your audio down to the Timeline. Instead of dragging it to the Video or Title Overlay tracks, drag it to the Audio/Music track. The song will appear as a rectangle on the Timeline and you can shorten it or move it around just as you would with a video clip.

4 Click on the **playback head** under the monitor window and you should be able to hear your music playing alongside the video.

Fading In and Out

Right now, the music starts and stops rather abruptly. To give it a smooth fade in and out, right click on the music in the **Timeline** and simply choose **Fade in** or **Fade out**.

Adjust the volume

It may well be when you play back the Timeline that the music is too loud and swamps the background sound of the video. This is easy to correct.

Go to the **Tools** menu and choose **Audio Levels**. You'll be presented with a simple slider allowing you to adjust the balance between sound from the video and sound from the music track.

Music on CD

If your songs are on CD, you'll need to transfer (or Rip) them onto your hard drive first.

1 Place your CD in the computer, then go to the **Computer** or **My Computer** link in your start menu. A window will appear listing your computer's disk drives.

2 Select your CD drive, then right click on it and choose **Explore**. A list of the tracks will appear. Right click on any one of them and choose the **Open With** > **Windows Media Player**. The song will start playing.

3 Now choose **Rip** from the menu at the top of the media player window. You will be presented with a list of tracks on the CD. Make sure the tick boxes to the left of the tracks you need are checked and then click the **Start Rip** button at the bottom right of the window.

4 In the box which appears, choose **No copy protection**. Check the box at the bottom of the window, then click **OK**.

WARNING: COPY PROTECTION Music is generally copyrighted by the artist, record company and composer. If you want to use music in your productions and they're going to be shown publicly (put on the Internet, for example) then you risk prosecution if you don't get permission from the copyright holders. One solution to this is to use royalty free music which you can buy (quite cheaply) from Internet sites like www.productiontrax.com

5 Your tracks will now be transferred to your PC. By default, the music will be placed in the **Music** folder within your **My Documents** folder. That's the folder that opens when you click on **Audio or Music** from Windows Movie Maker. However, if you've changed any default settings, you may need to search around to find where your tracks are.

Voiceover

Recording a voiceover for your video is just as easy as adding music so long as you have a working microphone plugged into your PC. Many laptops come with a mic included. You can buy a plug-in microphone very cheaply, and it will plug directly into the microphone or audio in socket on your PC (the socket is usually pink).

To record a voiceover

1 In Windows Movie Maker, go to the **Tools** menu and select **Narrate Timeline**. You'll be presented with a set of controls and a monitor on which you can watch the video as you speak.

2 Click on the **show options** link and check the **mute speakers** box. This prevents the sound from the video playing back while you record as this would be distracting and could interfere with the sound from the microphone.

3 To add a narration, simply drag the **playback head** to the point at which you want to start recording on the Timeline, click the **Start Narration** button and begin speaking. The video will play back as you record, so you'll know when to start and stop talking.

4 When you've finished, click **Stop Narration** and you'll be able to save your recording to disk. You can save your narration anywhere you like, but saving it in the same folder as your music or video clips helps to keep everything together.

5 When you close the narration window, you'll be taken back to the familiar editing view and your narration clip (or clips if you've recorded more than one) will be listed in the **Imported Media** window. They'll also have been placed onto the **Timeline** for you so you can simply play back your production.

As with music, you can adjust the balance of background sound and narration by selecting **Audio Levels** from the Tools menu.

TIPS: NARRATION

1 Don't add your narration until you've finished editing your video – if you change anything later, you'll have to do it again.

2 Know what you're going to say. Write a script if you need to and prop it up so that you can read easily from it without rustling paper

3 You can do as many takes as you like, so don't worry about messing it up. You can save each take with a different name or, if you don't like a take, you don't have to save it at all.

4 Test your sound levels. Place the microphone close, but not too close, and adjust the levels setting on the screen so that when you speak normally the level indicator flickers in the green or yellow area, but never peaks into the red.

5 Watch your video playing back and time your words to go along with the pictures. Don't be afraid to pause or vary the speed of your speech.

6 If you record several versions of your voiceover, you can combine them by simply dropping them onto the Timeline and then trimming each one to size so that only the best sections of each are heard.

EFFECTS

In Chapter 5 we tried out some special effects to create movement on still images. Windows Movie Maker also includes some extra effects designed to jazz up moving footage.

Adding effects

1 To add a special effect to a clip on the **Timeline**, go to the **Edit** menu at the left of the screen and select **effects**.

2 Drag the effect of your choice to the **Timeline** and release it over the clip you want to affect.

3 You'll then be able to view the effect by playing back the Timeline.

TIP: KEEPING TRACK OF YOUR EFFECTS

You can easily see which clips on the Timeline have effects applied to them from the silver star icon displayed on the clip.

HINT: ADDING EXTRA EFFECTS

You can apply more than one effect to the same clip. If you do, the clip may play back jerkily on the Timeline, but this won't affect your finished movie. The jerkiness is simply because the computer has to apply all your effects to every frame before playing it.

Managing your effects

1 You can see what effects you've applied to a clip and alter them by right clicking on the clip and selecting **Effects**.

2 This brings up a **Add or Remove Effects** window with all the available effects listed down the left hand side and all the ones you're currently using indicated on the right.

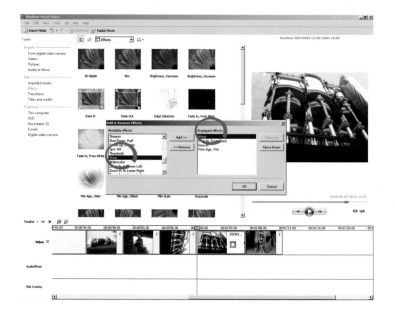

You can select and add or remove effects quickly and easily in this window.

You can also move them up or down the right-hand list. The order in which effects are applied does make a difference. For example, if you apply a **film grain** effect followed by a **blur effect**, then the grain will be blurred. If you arrange the effects so that the blur comes first, then the clip will be blurred but the grain will be sharp.

Effects available in Windows Movie Maker

Here are a few of the program's effects with a brief description of their results:

3D Ripple and Warp
Wobbles the shot as though it's being filmed reflected in rippling water

Blur
Adds a slight blur to de-focus the clip. If you want more of a blur, simply add more blur effects

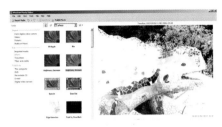

Brightness increase/decrease
Dims or brightens the clip slightly

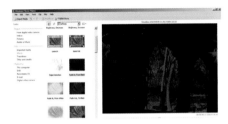

Fade In/Out
Fades the shot in or out from white or black at the beginning or end.

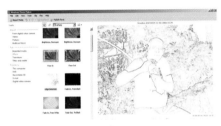

Edge Detection
Creates a stencil effect.

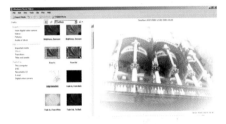

Film Age/ Film Grain
Four different effects for creating an old film style by adding grain, flickers and film damage.

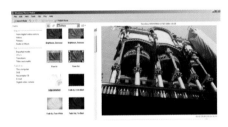

Grey Scale and Sepia tone
Turns your shot to black and white or sepia

Hue Cycles
Progressively changes the colour of your shot over the course of the clip

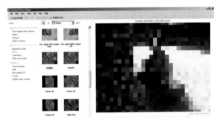

Pixellate
Turns your image into a mosaic

Posterise and Watercolour
Give the shot a hand-painted look

Slow Down and Speed Up
Create slow and fast motion effects

Sharpen
Highlights the detail in your image. Can be useful on some out of focus shots, but it won't perform miracles

8 Publishing your videos

Once your video production has been edited, you'll want to allow people to watch it. Recently, video players have been popping up everywhere. As well as being able to watch a DVD video on your TV, you can watch it on your PC, over the Internet, or even on a mobile phone or a portable music player such as the ipod.

All these different ways of watching require different types of video. DVD footage is great quality, but because of that its files are too big to play over the Internet. Mobile phone video is great if you're on the move, but the screen is a different shape to your TV.

For each format, then, you need to create your video in a slightly different way. Luckily, Windows Movie Maker allows you to produce all kinds of video programmes fairly easily.

MAKING A VIDEO TO PLAY ON YOUR COMPUTER

 MAKE A BACKUP COPY FIRST It's always a good idea – especially when you've put a lot of work into a video – to start by creating a backup copy for your computer. You can keep this on your hard drive and play it back whenever you want.

1 Load up Windows Movie Maker and go to the **Publish to** menu at the left of the screen. Select the **This computer** link; you'll then be asked where you want the file saved to and what you want it to be called.

2 When you've chosen, click **Next** and you'll be given a choice of different quality options. It's usually best to stick to the default option.

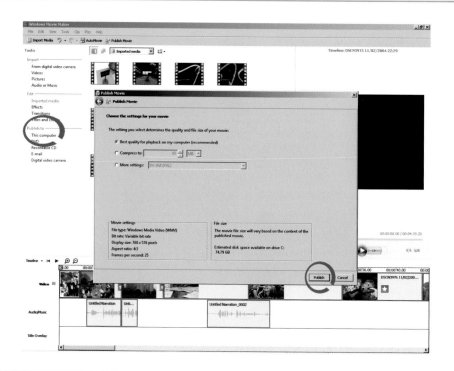

HINT: CREATING SMALLER FILES

The **Compress to** option allows you to create a file of a size you specify, but bear in mind that the smaller the file, the more the video will be compressed and the worse the quality will be. The **more settings** option allows you to select from a series of presets designed for creating specific types of file, and the box at the bottom of the screen gives information on exactly what kind of output you'll get if you select the various options. If you decide to pick your own preset, make sure you take notice of the **frame size**, **estimated file-size** and number of **frames per second**.

3 After you've selected your file type, click **Publish** to create your finished movie. At this point, the computer has to go through every frame of your movie, adding any effects and then re-compressing the video into the required format. The progress bar shows how long this will take, but if you're making a long video, you should expect your PC to be tied up for several hours.

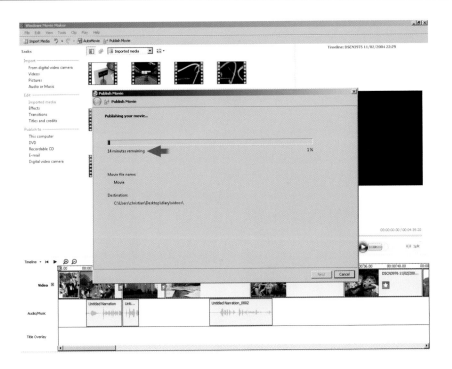

4 Once the work is done, you can play back your file without loading Windows Movie Maker: simply locate the file using **Computer** or **My computer** and double click on it.

MAKING A VIDEO FOR A MOBILE PHONE OR IPOD

Video ipods, in common with most other handheld video players and almost all video enabled mobile phones, play videos using a special format known as mp4 (mp3 is for music, mp4 is for video). These files are very well compressed, so you can fit a lot into a small space and they play back well on most devices.

Hand-held video player

Windows Movie Maker can't create an mp4 video on its own, but there is free software available which will convert Windows Movie Maker's files into mp4 format in a few simple steps.

Here, we'll be using Jodix free ipod video converter – a very simple little utility which will transfer pretty much any video to mp4 format.

1   Start by publishing a version of your video from Windows Movie Maker to your computer, just as you did on page 70.

2   Now, close Windows Movie Maker and open Jodix. Select **Add files** and locate the video file you've just created.

3   A window will display the video's name along with some other details. Simply click **Next** and select the recommended option from the **Video size** dropdown list. Go to **Output file** and choose a location for storing your converted video clip.

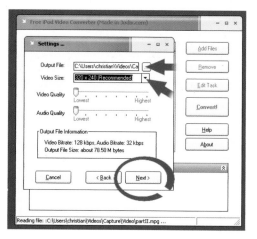

4   Click **Next** again and you can fill in a title for your movie along with some additional details. These aren't necessary, but they'll help you find the video on your ipod or other device if you've got a lot of files on there already.

5   Click **OK** and you'll be returned to the main screen. The great thing about Jodix is that you can add as many files as you like and they'll be converted one after another. This means that you can line up as many clips as you like and leave the PC to convert them on its own while you do something else.

6   Finally, click **Convert!** and your videos will be re-created in mp4 format without damaging the original versions.

You can now use the software that came with your video device (if it's an ipod, it will be iTunes) to transfer the footage onto your hand-held video player.

UPLOADING YOUR VIDEO TO THE INTERNET

Now that most people have broadband Internet connections, it has become possible for video to be played over the Internet at a watchable quality. This has led to a huge explosion in online video sites. The most famous of these is YouTube, but there are many others. These sites allow you to upload videos and make them available for anyone to watch from anywhere in the world.

The process is quick and easy and you can use it (for example) to allow friends and relatives anywhere in the world to see a clip of your wedding or birthday party videos – or you can create a documentary about something you feel passionately about and spread the word to anyone who cares to watch.

You then add keywords to your video to allow people searching the website to find your creation among the thousands of videos uploaded every day.

KEYWORDS

Keywords (or **Tags** as they're called on YouTube) are your main tool for getting your video seen online. Put simply, you select a number of words or phrases which relate to the content of your video and type them into a form on the website. When people search for videos – either through a search engine like Google or through a website's own search tools – they will type in words connected to whatever they're interested in seeing. If your video's keywords match the keywords they search for, your video will come up.

Of course, if your keywords are popular ones, there could be many thousands of results and your video may be a long way down the list, so it's up to you to choose the most effective and specific keywords you can. Just entering *seaside* will mean your video appears alongside a hundred thousand others involving the seaside. Entering a specific seaside location will mean it appears less often because not so many people will be searching for those words, but when it does appear, the chances are it will be exactly what the searcher is looking for.

You need to think about keywords and get a balance between general terms and more specific descriptions. Entering *seaside* and *Brighton* and *pier* separately would mean your video appeared on a lot of general searches as well as being well targeted for very specific requests. Of course, if you do that and your seaside video doesn't feature Brighton Pier, you'll just end up annoying people!

Search systems are very complex and often employ artificial intelligence, so a lot of factors go into deciding where in the list of results your video appears. However you'll often find videos that have been highly rated by other visitors or those that have had a lot of visitors already appearing higher up the list of search results.

Internet video sites all have their own uploading procedures, but there are features common to all. The first step is always to use Windows Movie Maker to create a video file that's good quality, but small enough to upload in a reasonable amount of time.

Uploading to YouTube

 USE A BROADBAND CONNECTION Uploading videos to the Internet can be very time consuming and it's not advisable to try it using a dial-up connection. If you only have a dial-up connection, save this tutorial until you have access to broadband.

1 From Windows Movie Maker, select **Publish to** > **This Computer** to create a video just as you did above. This time, however, go to the **more settings** option and select **windows media portable device**.

2 Create a YouTube account. Go to **www.youtube.com** and click the **Sign Up** link at the top right hand corner of the screen. You'll have to fill out a simple form before you can start uploading videos. It's up to you how much or little information you provide about yourself.

3 Go to the top left-hand of the screen and click on the **Upload** link. You'll then be able to provide information about your video including a title, a brief description and **tags** (keywords).

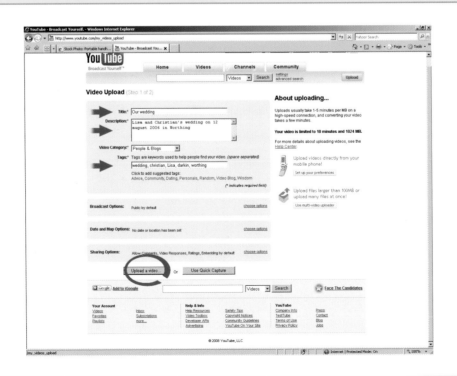

4 When you've filled out the information, click the **Upload a video** button and you'll be able to locate and upload your video (YouTube restricts videos to 10 minutes in length and 1gb in size).

5 You'll be informed when uploading has finished (it could take a long time, especially if you're using a slow connection). A few minutes after the upload has finished, the video will have been processed by YouTube's software and will be ready to view.

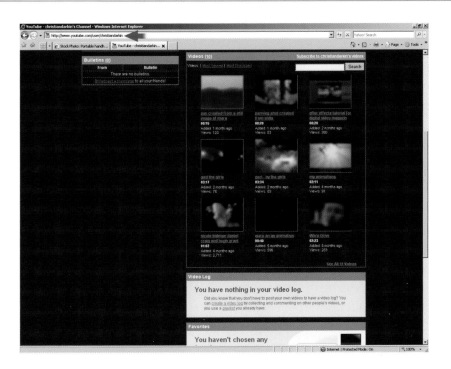

6 You can view your own videos from your profile page. If you want to email other people to let them know where to find your video, just click in the address line at the top of your browser window, select the entire address, then copy and paste it into your email (use Ctrl + C and Ctrl + V to copy and paste).

You can see how many times your video has been viewed, and visitors can add their own comments underneath the video clip.

CREATING A DVD

Making a DVD playable on a domestic DVD player is a great way to distribute your video to family and friends. Windows Movie Maker won't create DVDs by itself, but does load up another simple package automatically to create the disk for you.

1 From Windows Movie Maker, go to the **Publish** menu at the left of the screen and click on the **DVD** link. If you haven't already saved your production, you'll be prompted to do so. **Windows DVD Maker** will now load and your movie will automatically be placed in a DVD project. Type a title for the disk in the field at the bottom of the window.

TIP: MULTIPLE MOVIES

If you want to, you can now use the **Add Items** button and import more movies to place on the same disk. The pie chart at the bottom left of the window lets you know how much space will be left on the disk when you burn it.

2 Click **Next** and you can choose a menu style for your DVD. Various layouts are arranged down the right-hand side of the window, and by simply clicking on one you can preview it in the main window. If you want to see how the menu will work once the disk is burned, click the **preview** button above the main window.

3 You can change the look of the menu by clicking on the **Menu text** button (next to **preview** at the top of the screen). This allows you to customise the font and colour as well as editing the on-screen text. When you have finished click **Change text**.

4 The **Customise menu** button allows you to choose styles for the **scenes button**, but also allows you to change the video clip that plays in the background of the menu (you can load in a still picture if you prefer) and the foreground video clip. Click **Change style** to apply.

5 You can also choose a piece of music from your hard drive to play in the background while your viewer chooses what to watch from the menu. Remember, this audio will be looped, so pick something that doesn't start and end too abruptly.

6 Finally, insert a blank disk in your DVD burner and press the **Burn** button at the bottom right of the screen. Once it's finished you should be able to play the disk on most DVD players.

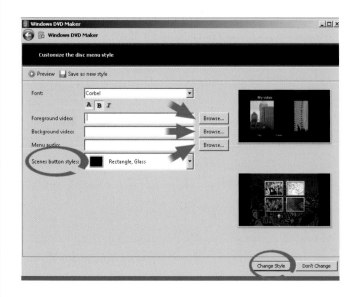

NOTE: PLAYING YOUR DVDS Some people have reported problems playing home-burned DVDs on their domestic players. This is usually to do with compatibility problems between the make of DVD burner, the disks used and the DVD player they're played on. If you have trouble, try different combinations of players and disks to find out what works for you.

CLEANING UP YOUR HARD DRIVE

Digital video can end up taking up a huge amount of space on your computer and after you've finished editing a project, you probably won't want to keep all the original footage files clogging up your PC.

1 Once you've created your final edit, create a high quality master copy (see page 70), as you may want to make more copies of your video in the future. You can then delete all your unwanted footage files.

2 Close down Windows Movie Maker and select **Computer** or **My Computer** from your start menu. If you've put your video footage in a particular folder, navigate to it now. If you haven't, Windows Movie Maker will have placed it in your **My Documents** folder. Locate your **Documents** or **My Documents** folder (in the top left of the browser screen) and find the Videos folder within it.

3 Examine the files kept here and work out which ones are the footage for your finished project. Select them all (hold down Ctrl while you click) and hit the Del key. Select **yes** to confirm the move.

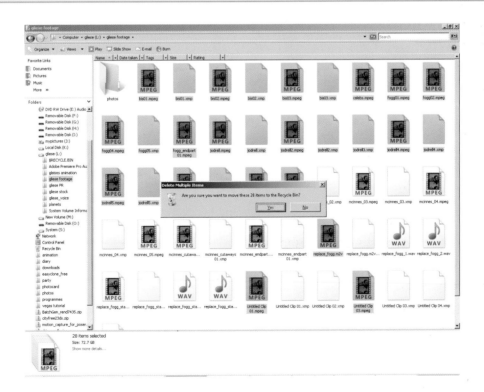

4 When you're sure you've removed all the files and made certain that you haven't deleted anything you'll need, go to the **recycle bin** on your **desktop** and empty it.

WAIT BEFORE YOU EMPTY YOUR RECYCLE BIN It's usually best to wait a couple of weeks between deleting your files and emptying the recycle bin just in case you've deleted something you wanted to keep, or you decide you want to make amendments to your edited work. If this happens, you can simply open the recycle bin, select the deleted items and select Restore.

ADVANCED EDITING PACKAGES

If you want to take your Digital Video editing a little further, you may want to move beyond what Windows Movie Maker can do. There is a range of much more powerful editing packages available which will allow you to edit with more precision, add more complex cuts, and work with extra effects. Here are a few examples:

| Pinnacle Studio | Adobe Premiere Elements |

Pinnacle Studio – a very easy to use layout combined with some useful one-click solutions to common editing problems such as poor quality sound and shaky camera work.

Adobe Premiere Elements – a slightly more involved package, but one with a wider range of effects and a set of editing tools very similar to those used in professional edit suites.

Videowave – a package which concentrates on simplicity of use, but comes bundled with lots of other useful software for photo editing, archiving and other common tasks. Very easy-to-use layout combined with some useful one-click solutions to common editing problems such as poor quality sound and shaky camera work.

Throughout this book, we've discovered how to seek out the best shots and collect the material needed for a great video production. We've learned to import the raw footage from camcorders, mobile phones and still cameras into our computer, and from there, we've cut that footage into scenes designed to tell interesting stories. We've even learned how to add narration, music, titles and effects to our work. In this final chapter, we've produced our finished video in a range of formats from DVD right through to broadcast on the Internet.

You'll never stop learning about video production, and the more you shoot, the better your work will become. Video is the medium of the future, and the best way to learn it is to shoot and edit as much as you can and as often as you can. So fire up your PC, pick up your camera, and hit the big, red record button.

INDEX

NEW HOLLAND

First published in 2009 by New Holland Publishers (UK) Ltd
London · Cape Town · Sydney · Auckland

Garfield House
86–88 Edgware Road
London, W2 2EA
United Kingdom
www.newhollandpublishers.com

80 McKenzie Street
Cape Town 8001
South Africa

Unit 1, 66 Gibbes Street
Chatswood, NSW 2067
Australia

218 Lake Road
Northcote, Auckland
New Zealand

1 3 5 7 9 10 8 6 4 2
ISBN 978 1 84773 423 5

Editors: Barbara Cooke and Amy Corstorphine
Design: AG&G Books
Production: Laurence Poos
DTP: Peter Gwyer
Editorial Direction: Rosemary Wilkinson

Printed and bound by Times Offset, Malaysia

Acknowledgements

Microsoft, Encarta, MSN, and Windows are either registered trademarks or trademarks of Microsoft Corporation
in the United States and/or other countries. Microsoft product screenshots reprinted with permission from
Microsoft Corporation. **Photo Credits**: Cover, p.11 (top) JVC, p.7, 9 (bottom left), p.10 (top right), p.11 (centre)
Canon; p.8 (Top left) Mustek; p.8 (top centre and right) Fuji; p.14 (bottom) © Constantin Opris/Dreamstime.com;
p.22 © Pippawest/Dreamstime.com; p.23 (top) © Demonike/Dreamstime.com;
p.23 bottom © Iofoto/Dreamstime.com; p.24 © Deshacam/Dreamstime.com;
p.26 and 28 © Colicaranica/Dreamstime.com; p.27 © Niderlander/Dreamstime.com;
p.29 top © Stuartkey/Dreamstime.com; p.29 bottom © Aleandr/Dreamstime.com